A Soldier's Sketch-book

With the British Army in the Gulf 1990-91

by
Robin Watt

Frontispiece. Major Robin Watt, Royal Hussars,
sketching Challenger tanks of the Royal Scots Dragoon Guards
at live firing practice on Devil Dog Dragoon Range, Abu Hadriyah,
Saudi Arabia, 2 January 1991

© Laurie Manton

A Soldier's Sketch-book

With the British Army in the Gulf 1990-91

by
Robin Watt

Published to coincide with the Special Exhibition
of the Artist's watercolours and drawings
held at the National Army Museum
13 October 1994 - 12 February 1995

A National Army Museum Publication

A Soldier's Sketch-book

With the British Army in the Gulf 1990-91

by
Robin Watt

Edited by Michael Ball

Designed by Derek Buick

Photography by Nigel Armstrong, Ian Jones
and Karen Millar

Cover picture: 'Going Home'. Tank crews of C Squadron,
The Queen's Royal Irish Hussars, 'de-bombing' (unloading ammunition from)
their Challenger tanks at Al Jubayl, Saudi Arabia, 13 March 1991

Printed in Great Britain by Sterling Press

To the British soldiers who took part
in Operation GRANBY and their families.
In my own case, this means, in particular,
Jane, Rosie, and Robin

RW

CONTENTS

FOREWORD

The Gulf War of 1990-91 saw the British Army play a leading role in one of the most successful operations in the history of armoured warfare. Its remarkable achievement is a testimony not only to the skills and commitment of the 35,000 Army personnel who served in the Gulf, but also to the Royal Navy and RAF Forces, and many others working in the United Kingdom, Germany, and elsewhere.

The National Army Museum is concerned as much with the present-day activities of the British Army as with its past and indeed, shortly after hostilities ended, two members of the Museum staff travelled to the Gulf region to collect material. This resulted in the nucleus of the Museum's Gulf War Collection, which comprises everything from armoured fighting vehicles to plastic cutlery.

The Gulf Conflict was the subject of unprecedented media attention, and few will forget the images which appeared nightly on their television screens. For one individual however, the War provided the opportunity for a very different kind of record. Major Robin Watt, then serving with the Royal Hussars (Prince of Wales's Own), chose as his medium a pencil and sketch-book, and obtained permission to travel to Saudi Arabia to join the 7th Armoured Brigade, principally as an artist. He remained with the Brigade throughout its training build-up, and later accompanied The Queen's Royal Irish Hussars Battle Group during the ground offensive, Operation DESERT SABRE.

It was a task for which he was exceptionally well-qualified. Robin Watt had spent his school holidays in Iraq, where both his Father and Grandfather lived and worked. This laid the foundations of a lasting and informed interest in the Islamic world. Throughout his Army career he had also pursued a keen interest in drawing, in particular, birds and animals.

Robin Watt dislikes the term 'war artist'; he is perhaps best seen as part of the long tradition of soldier-artists, stretching back to the early nineteenth century, whose work forms one of the most important parts of the Museum's Art Collection. These pictures are especially important because, like Robin Watt, these artists had a professional understanding of the subject matter which they recorded.

The National Army Museum is pleased to be able to bring together the results of this Soldier-Artist's work in the Gulf as a Special Exhibition. Firstly, a selection of some of his original field sketches and loose drawings, which he has generously donated to the Museum. Secondly, the display includes a number of finished works produced since the end of the Gulf

Conflict. Additionally, in *A Soldier's Sketch-book*, the Artist's own account of his time in the Gulf, drawn from his diaries and letters home, is published for the first time. Illustrated with a selection of his sketches and finished works, it is a unique record, not only of the activities of the British Army, but also of the people of the Gulf region and their environment. It is hoped that it will give much pleasure to those who enjoy Robin Watt's pictures.

Apart from the sketch-books and drawings donated by the Artist to the National Army Museum, most of the material in this Special Exhibition comes from his own collection. In addition to those who prefer to remain anonymous and cannot be thanked by name, I should like to express the Museum's gratitude to the following, who have lent material; the Regimental Headquarters, Irish Guards, by kind permission of Lieutenant-Colonel S J L Roberts OBE; 4th (County Fermanagh and County Tyrone) Battalion, The Royal Irish Regiment, by kind permission of Lieutenant-Colonel W R Harber MBE; The Royal Logistic Corps; The Intelligence Corps; and Simon Dunstan. We are grateful to Laurie Manton for permission to reproduce the frontispiece, and to Jane Winspear for additional research.

In addition to the members of staff of the National Army Museum credited on the title page, thanks are also due to the following for their help in the preparation of this book; Alan Guy, June Hicks, Kate Plowman, and Jenny Spencer-Smith. The Special Exhibition at the National Army Museum, which this book complements, was organized by Michael Ball with the assistance of the following staff; Emma Armstrong, Derek Buick, Adrian Carlton, Sarah Godwin, Alice Lewis, Ray Seabrook, and Paul Tew. It is open to visitors from 13 October 1994 to 12 February 1995.

Ian G Robertson   National Army Museum
Director   September 1994

PREFACE

It was the 7th Armoured Brigade's good fortune that we were asked to employ Major Robin Watt in November 1990. He came to the Gulf to fight and also to record, through his drawings, a brief moment in history.

And like many of us he kept a diary. These will all record a war that, as with others, contained mistakes and human frailty, a war in which each man's tent or foxhole was a private battlefield of concern and emotion.

Robin Watt's writings are unique because of the addition of beautiful, painstakingly detailed drawings which help the reader not only to understand the curious conditions in which we lived for six months, but also the sights we saw during and after the battle. For me they are powerful reminders of dramatic and peaceful moments, in many ways far more vivid than the written word or photographs.

This work also highlights the strange juxtaposition of beauty and horror that becomes familiar to soldiers in war. The sketches of dawn and sunset in the desert, timelessly beautiful, lie uneasily next to pictures of casualties and destruction. Fortunately time moves on, the scorpions and jerboas did survive and the oil well fires were extinguished; the natural world recovered.

Robin Watt's work, a lasting evidence of his talents, will be much appreciated by all of us who were there and also by those wishing to understand the nature and atmosphere of warfare.

Major-General P A J Cordingley DSO   March 1994

ACKNOWLEDGEMENTS

I would like to thank the many members of the 7th Armoured Brigade who have helped me in my task. I refer, in particular, to Brigadier P A J Cordingley (now Major-General P A J Cordingley DSO) for his advice on the structure of this book, and for ensuring that I remained in the Gulf with the 7th Armoured Brigade when I should have been elsewhere.

I would also like to thank the Officers, Non-Commissioned Officers and soldiers of The Queen's Royal Irish Hussars Battle Group who so generously and courteously gave me a home. Here I refer, in particular, to Colonel Arthur Denaro (now Brigadier A G Denaro OBE), who so clearly understood the spirit of my venture, and his Second-in-Command, Major Mark O'Reilly who, when the vexed question arose for the 7th Armoured Brigade Staff, of exactly where I should be placed within the Brigade organization, decided the issue with the words, 'he is coming with us!'. For this, and for the innumerable ways in which he has helped me over the past four years, I owe Mark O'Reilly a special debt.

I also owe much to Major David Swann, who allowed my attachment to his squadron, B Squadron The Queen's Royal Irish Hussars, during Operation DESERT SABRE, and to Captain Johnny Ormerod of the same squadron. I thank them both, heartily, for their grace at such a busy and uncertain time. So too Captain Richard Bryson, Royal Regiment of Artillery, and Captain Tony Hood, 5th Inniskilling Dragoon Guards, whose Warriors I shared during the battle.

I also wish to thank Mrs Margaret Knott who, with charm and patience, somehow managed to decipher my field diaries to produce the original typescript. My immediate family apart, I owe much to the unstinting support of my mother, Mrs A E M Watt, my sister Caroline Zvegintzov and my brother-in-law, Lieutenant-Colonel Ivan Zvegintzov.

Finally, I would like to thank those members of the National Army Museum staff who have contributed so excellently to this project. I refer, in particular, to Dr Alan Guy, Jenny Spencer-Smith, and my editor, Michael Ball, who have, together, assembled this account with such care and sensitivity.

RW

LIST OF ILLUSTRATIONS

Front Cover

'Going Home'. Tank crews of C Squadron, The Queen's Royal Irish Hussars,'de-bombing' (unloading ammunition from) their Challenger tanks at Al Jubayl, Saudi Arabia, 13 March 1991

Frontispiece

Robin Watt sketching Challenger tanks of the Royal Scots Dragoon Guards at live firing practice on Devil Dog Dragoon Range, Abu Hadriyah, Saudi Arabia, 2 January 1991

Back Cover
Robin Watt sketching at Al Fadhili, Saudi Arabia, 30 December 1990

GLOSSARY OF TERMS AND ABBREVIATIONS

1 Staffords	1st Battalion, The Staffordshire Regiment
17/21L	17th/21st Lancers
ADTR	Armoured Division Transport Regiment
ANGLICO	Air and Naval Gunfire Liaison Company
APC	Armoured Personnel Carrier
APU	Auxiliary Power Unit
AWACS	Airborne Warning and Control System
BDA	Battle Damage Assessment
Berm	A protective bank of earth
BW	Biological Warfare
Casevac	Casualty evacuation
CET	Combat Engineer Tractor
Compo	Composite rations (usually dehydrated)
DS	Dressing Station
Fin	Armour-Piercing Fin-Stabilized Discarding Sabot (ammunition)
FMA	Force Maintenance Area
FOO	Forward Observation Officer
FRG	Forward Repair Group
FTX	Field Training Exercise
FUP	Forming Up Place
HEAT	High Explosive Anti-Tank (ammunition)
HESH	High Explosive Squash Head (ammunition)
IV	Intravenous (drip)
KKMC	King Khalid's Military City
KTO	Kuwait Theatre of Operations
MEF	Marine Expeditionary Force
MLRS	Multiple Launch Rocket System
MRG	Medium Repair Group
MSR	Main Supply Route
NAPS	Nerve Agent Pills
NBC	Nuclear, Biological and Chemical (warfare)
O Group	Orders Group
Op	Operation
Psyops	Psychological Operations
POW	Prisoner of War
QDG	1st The Queen's Dragoon Guards

QRIH	The Queen's Royal Irish Hussars
Recce	Reconnaissance
RA	Royal Regiment of Artillery
RE	Corps of Royal Engineers
REME	Corps of Royal Electrical and Mechanical Engineers
RGFC	Republican Guard Force Command
RHA	Royal Horse Artillery
RHQ	Regimental Headquarters
RSM	Regimental Sergeant-Major
RV	Rendezvous
SAM	Surface-to-Air Missile
Scots DG	Royal Scots Dragoon Guards
TOGS	Thermal Observation and Gunnery Sight

Operation Codenames

DESERT SHIELD	Early defensive operations in Saudi Arabia
DESERT STORM	The offensive operation to liberate Kuwait
DESERT SWORD	The land operation to liberate Kuwait
DESERT SABRE	1st (BR) Armoured Division's contribution to DESERT SWORD
GRANBY	The British contribution to operations in the Gulf

Editor's Note

The text of this book is taken mostly from Robin Watt's field diaries, but also includes extracts from letters home which are printed in italics and appear next to the diary entries of the same date. Letters to the artist's mother, Mrs A E M Watt, are identified; all others were written to the artist's wife, Jane. Explanatory notes within the text appear in square brackets.

INTRODUCTION

It was my privilege and great good fortune to be attached to the 7th Armoured Brigade for Operation GRANBY from 28 November 1990 to 15 March 1991, and to The Queen's Royal Irish Hussars Battle Group from 4 January to 15 March 1991. My principal role was that of artist. My additional role was purely military and quite separate. Both periods included the preparation phase for Operation DESERT SABRE, and Operation DESERT SABRE itself. During the latter I took part in the advance of the 7th Armoured Brigade travelling in a Warrior of B Squadron The Queen's Royal Irish Hussars.

My overall purpose was to produce a record of the 7th Armoured Brigade and its supporting elements, in order to raise money for the Army Benevolent Fund. As a soldier I find myself instinctively avoiding the popular term 'war artist', which I find repugnant. My purpose was simply to record whatever I found, by means of field sketches and written text. The central core of this text is taken from a diary and letters written at the time.

The field sketches were not originally intended for public view. Later, I decided to include some of them, as no subsequent work, made in the comfort of a studio, can ever match the immediacy of drawings and field notes made on the spot, however sparse the result may be. I stress therefore that the field sketches are simply the germ of ideas for subsequent paintings, a form of pictorial shorthand, the sole purpose of which is to trigger the memory. Most of these sketches are unfinished, some consist of just a few lines, others are hardly more than scribbles. A few, made during Operation DESERT SABRE, were drawn at night in almost pitch darkness, in sandstorms or driving rain, almost without being able to see either the point of the pencil or the paper on which the sketch was made. Nevertheless, I always worked on the principle that something was better than nothing. *My* enemy was time and the elements, but I did the best I could in the time I had. Since the end of Operation GRANBY I have used these 'raw' field sketches to produce some properly finished work, with images that I hope some may recognize!

In essence, I have tried to capture the flavour of living, training, and fighting in the desert at crew level. I have also commented on the aftermath of the Gulf War, the images of which will remain forever with those who saw them. Ironically, of all sections of society, it is probably the soldier himself who views the effects of war with the greatest revulsion. Consequently, as time passes, I expect we will dwell less on its destructive aspect and more on its antithesis; those sometimes surprising qualities of human nature that provide a balance and give us cause for hope: respect, selflessness, humour, dignity, compassion, patience, humility, and great comradeship, to name but a few. These traditional, but perhaps less obvious, qualities of the

British soldier I saw again and again as I went about with sketch-pad and pencil. Naturally, some of these qualities are barely visible in peacetime and only emerge with full intensity when the clutter of life has been cut away.

But this is not purely a military record. Indeed, I would not be content if it were. Instead I have set my observations not in isolation, but in their correct context against the background of Arabia. I do not pretend to be an expert on the Middle East, but I have had the good fortune to have lived in Iraq. I have also visited a number of other Arab or Arabic-speaking countries and developed a deep interest in this fascinating region. Consequently, I have tried to provide at least a glimpse of Arabia including the nature of its people, its immense contribution to Western culture, and its place in history. This is important because, as always, history has a bearing on the present and the events of the Gulf War are no exception. I have also added some explanatory notes, researched in retrospect, on a number of non-military aspects of desert life. These range from date palms to camels, and seek to explain some of the things we may have seen, usually for only a moment, as we moved about the desert.

Robin Watt
Bovington
January 1993

CHAPTER ONE
Iraq - A Memory

I have a direct connection with Iraq, for three generations of my family have lived there. My grandfather, Major C R Chadwick, lived in Baghdad for 40 years, where he became the Director-General of Veterinary Services. His work, for which he was was appointed CBE, involved, among other things, scientific research into bilharzia. He also played a prominent role in providing remounts for British Forces during the First World War. My mother spent most of her early life in Baghdad; my father, Lieutenant-Colonel W G Watt, fought with the 4th Indian Division during the Second World War. He also served with the Persia and Iraq Force (or Paiforce), based in Iraq, the purpose of which was to prevent a possible German offensive into the Mesopotamian region via the Caucasus. After the War my father served with the British Military Mission to Iraq until the assassination of King Faisal II in 1958. The political upheaval which followed severed my family's connection with the country.

I also lived in Baghdad, where I spent my school holidays, but my strongest memories are of the harsh beauty of the desert. I often accompanied my father, who was a keen shot, on expeditions to the huge alluvial flood plain that stretches between the Tigris and Euphrates rivers from Hit and Samarra, west of Baghdad, to the Persian Gulf. In winter this region becomes one of the largest wildfowl wetlands on earth, and I recall seeing birds in vast numbers against a background of spectacular dawns and dusks. Countless numbers of duck, mainly mallard and teal, wheeled over the *jheels* (marshes), and snipe abounded. Most memorable of all were the long, rippling lines on the horizon which signalled the presence of geese on the move in many thousands, sweeping in from Siberia to winter in Iran and the marshes of Iraq.

Our expeditions began well before dawn. We would speed through sleeping villages along the empty roads that led from Baghdad towards Hillah. The mud-brick villages were built on mounds, the roads on embankments, raised high above the floods that afflict central and lower Iraq in the spring of most years, transforming this part of Mesopotamia into one vast sheet of water. Sometimes we glimpsed a camel or caught a jackal's eyes glowing in the headlights. Still in darkness, we would leave the roadside, to pick our way on foot across the *jheel* to a suitable spot beneath a flight line and lie in wait below a *bund*, the raised earth bank of an irrigation ditch. It was bitterly cold, and ice cracked and splintered under foot. We would hear the geese call or see them settle in great gatherings far out on the marsh. Sometimes we stalked them along the *bunds* and, just occasionally, we managed to steal among these extraordinarily wary creatures. Then a great roar would break and the whole surface of the marsh seemed to rise in the air. The geese turned and were gone.

We led a colonial-style life in the Alwiyah district of Baghdad, where large whitewashed bungalows with verandahs stood amongst a profusion of trees, flowering shrubs, and shaded lawns watered by a network of irrigation ditches. Hedges of oleander grew amongst mulberry trees, vines, and eucalyptus. Marigolds, zinnias, and lemon-scented verbena thrived alongside gourds and other trailing creepers. Hoopoes and turtle doves were a common sight, as were turkeys from Kurdistan, held captive on the flat rooftops of bungalows and fattened for Christmas on a diet of walnuts. Our staff were a motley band, friendly and willing. We had an Indian bearer, an Armenian gardener, an Assyrian *syce* groom), and a Goanese cook. There was also a night-watchman who patrolled the bungalows.

The artist with his mother, Mrs A E M Watt, sister Caroline, and 'Billy', in the garden of their family home in the Alwiyah district of Baghdad, 1956

In summer, when temperatures occasionally soared to 120 degrees Fahrenheit [49°C] in the shade, we would swim at the Alwiyah Club to escape the wilting heat. Indian and Armenian bearers scurried about with trays laden with tall glasses misted with condensation and filled with fizzy drinks. I remember well the purr of the air conditioner as I stepped from the summer heat into the cool of our bungalow. The air conditioner was a simple device consisting of a water-tank attached to the outside of the bungalow on a raised platform, with an electric fan that drove cool air into the rooms. The air was cooled by evaporation accelerated by the desert winds - the dry, gusting, southerly *sharqi* of early summer or the prevailing northerly wind of mid-summer, the *shamaal*, that blows steadily until early autumn.

In winter we would go racing at the Al Mansur course, where my grandfather was both judge and handicapper. On other occasions I would accompany him on visits to the Royal Stables to register young Arabian racehorses, one small aspect of his work as a veterinary surgeon. He would record their colour, age and measurements, and tattoo them to reduce their chances of being stolen, or switched on race days.

Beyond the green and restful sanctuary of Alwiyah lay the River Tigris and the sprawling city of Baghdad which reeked with the scents, sounds, and bustle of Arabia. I recall my fascination with the colour and chaos of Rashid Street with cars, carts, and lorries going in every direction with horns blaring. Figures hurried along, stood, or squatted in huddles chatting, smoking, or selling their wares. Everywhere there were blue beads, sewn into jewellery, bridles, or the skull-caps of children, or dangling on strings in the cabs of taxis as lucky charms to ward off the 'evil eye'. Water sellers refreshed dusty travellers from rows of *tungas*, the elegant, long-necked earthenware pots which kept water deliciously cool. Other traders offered lime tea, mint tea, sherbet or the fermented milk (of goats, cows, buffaloes or ewes) known locally as *leban* or *roba*. Startling displays of vegetables and fruit from this Garden of Eden were piled high by the side of the road: dates, oranges, lemons and limes; pomegranates and aubergines; apples from Kurdistan; tomatoes and water melons; and apricots and almonds, set against a backdrop of mosques and minarets. And then there was the covered *souk* (market) in the north of the city with its dealers in carpets, copper, spice, silk, gold, and precious stones.

Desert mosque, Al Fadhili, Saudi Arabia,
24 December 1990

But I was always struck by the stark contrasts of this harsh land. Baghdad was filled with the scent of coriander and cinnamon; of *couscous*, a thick lamb stew with a base of cracked wheat, usually served with the strong *harissa* pepper; of the unleavened bread *khubz*, the staple of the Iraqi diet; and with the aroma of the freshwater 'Tigris salmon' *masguf*, split in half, spitted and grilled over open fires. These smells mingled with the rank stench that rose from the River Tigris as it threaded its way through the heart of the city. Tiny children, deformed or with casts in their eyes, covered in 'Baghdad boils' and flies, begged in filth. Donkeys, always overladen, were hard-driven. *Arabanas*, or two-horse carriages, plied the streets dragged by emaciated animals with protruding ribs and covered in sores, some almost dead in the shafts. Packs of pye-dogs that roamed the streets were rounded up periodically and shot to curb the threat of rabies, usually transmitted by jackals. I learnt that this was the harsh reality of life, not only in Arabia, but in many other parts of the world where attitudes to life and death are quite different from our own. I expect that, to the Arab, the West often appears pampered, demanding, and spoiled.

Beyond the city, in the long summer months, there was little but shimmering heat and the unforgiving harshness of the landscape. But sometimes we journeyed from Baghdad along the rivers or across the desert. The murderous heat of summer, like a furnace blast, seemed to bleach the sky to pale violet and the land to grey-green and ochre. I recall bumping along dusty tracks rutted by the floods of spring, passing through mud-brick villages and patches of cultivation where date palms, vegetables, and orange trees grew along the water courses. Sometimes we saw fishermen, working with floating nets from rowing boats or *kalaks*, rafts of inflated skins lashed together with reeds.

From time to time we drove due west from Baghdad through Fallujah to the Royal Air Force base at Habbaniyah. Beyond lay the Janubiyah, a stony desert with little sand, broken in places by flat-topped buttes and wide *wadis* (watercourses), some of which are 200 miles long and carry the torrential winter rains to the Euphrates. Sometimes we journeyed northwards from Baghdad through the *liwa*, or district, of Diala to the oil town of Kirkuk, skirting the barren upland gravel desert of the Jezira which lies between the Upper Tigris and Euphrates valleys to the west. Between Kirkuk, Erbil, and Mosul, the undulating wheat fields are scattered with areas of stone and grassy mounds where the lost cities of ancient Assyria lie buried. It is here that the north-eastern highlands of Iraqi Kurdistan begin, a place of deep gorges and rugged mountains. The latter form part of the Zagros system and rise to 12,000 feet near the Turkish and Iranian borders. This is a region which has changed little over the centuries, with rocky streams, orchards, water-meadows, and red earth. Its villages are built on terraces clinging to hillsides covered in scrub oak, pink campion, and anemones, where fields of rice and mustard intermingle with wild hyacinths and iris.

By contrast, the south-eastern region of Iraq between Basra and the district of Maysan is marshland, a watery wilderness covering 6,000 square miles centred on the town of Al Qurnah where the Tigris and Euphrates join to become the Shatt-al-Arab waterway. The area consists of marsh, a labyrinth of water channels, islands of floating vegetation, and lakes, the largest of which is the Hawr al Hammar. This isolated fastness teems with fish and game, and is inhabited by numerous tribes, continuing to live much as they always have, on mud platforms, in houses built of reeds known as *mudhifs*. The Marsh Arabs grow rice, raise buffaloes, hunt wild boar and stalk wildfowl; they fish from coracles and reed boats known collectively as *majhouf*. Historically, the marshes have also provided a refuge for defeated people or a rallying point for resistance.

The same pattern of struggle continues to this day in a brutal suppression of the Shi'ites by a ruthless Ba'athist regime bent on gaining control of the marshes by any means. This includes gas and acid attack, the bombing and burning of villages, and even the systematic draining of the marshes in an attempt to deprive the Marsh Tribes of their very means of existence. This reflects a trend set in motion many centuries earlier, in which Iraq has suffered from repeated invasions by foreign armies, or provided a battleground for rival armies within her boundaries. It was curious that fate should dictate my return to this troubled land over 30 years later, but this time in a very different guise.

CHAPTER TWO
Build-up

Tuesday 27/Wednesday 28 November 1990 Received the order to move to Saudi Arabia at 1500 hours on 27 November.[1] Spent the night of 27/28 November packing frantically. Pure hell with mountains of equipment laid out on the drawing room floor; not only military equipment but art equipment too. The Lockheed Tri-Star flew from RAF Brize Norton to Al Jubayl direct.[2] From this point onwards events became blurred.

Thursday 29 November Thence to Camp 4 in Al Jubayl.[3] The moment I arrived there was a full NBC [Nuclear, Biological, and Chemical warfare] exercise under way. I had to find my equipment rapidly from my bags. On the way to breakfast spotted a creeping plant with oval-shaped leaves and a mauve flower similar to a convolvulus,[4] and a bush with a mixture of violet and white flowers. Flocks of sparrow-like birds flitted amongst the lower branches of the small, bushy trees nearby. Travelled to Al Jubayl port by road, passing a large petro-chemical works and some American surface-to-air missile launchers designed to defeat Scud incomers.[5] Went to the Force Maintenance Area at Old Port Barracks. Lunched there and then tried to get a desert camouflage outfit, which proved quite impossible, despite having been told in England that uniforms would be easy to obtain in Saudi Arabia! But I did obtain a staff list of 7th Armoured Brigade and its supporting elements which will form the basis of my plan of attack on the art project. I now have a room in Camp 4.

Friday 30 November Met Captain Johnnie Wade, Royal Highland Fusiliers, at breakfast. He is an artist and watch-keeper at Headquarters 7th Armoured Brigade. He showed me his watercolours and drawings. Now that I am recovering from the journey out I am starting to take stock of my surroundings. Made the following observations at Camp 4. Date palms are carefully nurtured and heavily watered;[6] there are low bushes with pink and orange flowers, and small fig-like trees with long fleshy leaves.[7] Spent the morning working out a programme for my visit to 7th Armoured Brigade, and the rest of the day packing for a month in the desert... *It is now ten o'clock at night. A Scots Dragoon Guard is playing his bagpipes! My surroundings - a camp of 2,000 men. We are not allowed to visit the town of Al Jubayl but we can drive to the port which is about ten miles away. Nothing much to see except missile launchers and petro-chemical works, and the brilliant emerald green of the Persian Gulf.*

Saturday 1 December Arrived at Headquarters 7th Armoured Brigade about 1900. The sun disappeared rapidly at about 1700 but the full moon makes it possible to see about 200 yards or perhaps a little more. There is an orange glow on the horizon which is the burn-off from the oil refineries at Al Jubayl. I am writing these notes lying in my sleeping bag... *There is a natural bond between everyone here and none of the irksome aspects of peacetime soldiering. Everyone is armed to the teeth. They are here to do the job and get home. Whatever happens it is a very interesting situation!!*

Sunday 2 December At 0730 the Iraqis fired three Scud missiles. We masked up in full NBC kit and remained at full alert for two hours. It transpired that the Scuds were conventional, not chemical, and that their target lay within Iraq. The purpose was presumably to test fire the weapon and to gauge the Allies' reaction. This is the first time that the British Army has been fully masked since the First World War. Certainly when we knew the Scuds had been fired we thought that war had come. A strange feeling. Saw a group of 40-50 camels near our tented camp today.

I am now in the desert with HQ 7th Armoured Brigade. I arrived yesterday just as the sun was going down. It disappears at a rate of knots once it is near the horizon. The moon rises simultaneously. At the moment it is full so it's possible to see about 300-400 yards, although not particularly distinctly. The sand is slightly orange in sunlight and bluish-green in shadow. There are clumps of camel-thorn and small black lava-like stones.[8] Otherwise nothing. It is not dead flat but slightly rolling. At night there is a glow on the horizon which is the smelting plant or petro-chemical works at Al Jubayl. I am glad I am away from Camp 4 which is crowded and very humid. The desert is perfectly dry. It gets very cold towards dawn. I wore two jerseys at daybreak today (two thick ones at that).

Monday 3 December Remained at Headquarters 7th Armoured Brigade in Nufayl training area. Received an intelligence brief. Included detailed estimates of the composition of the Iraqi divisions known to be concentrated in KTO [Kuwait Theatre of Operations] in terms of men, tanks, and artillery pieces. Also the nature of the obstacle belt in terms of mines, wire, berms [protective banks of earth], oil channels, and flame trenches.[9] Also the fact that the Iraqis are expected to fire the oil wells (each well-head can produce 1,500 degrees of heat) to impede an Allied advance, and other possible Iraqi plans to hinder amphibious troop landings on the Kuwaiti coast. The bulk of the Iraqi army is now deployed in Kuwait. Very few Iraqi units remain in Iraq. Re-supply and morale problems. Some humint [human intelligence] from Kuwaiti refugees and resistance fighters.

[Letter to Mrs A E M Watt] It is pretty hot from about 11-3. It then cools off. Dawn is freezing. The sunsets and moonrises are pretty spectacular. You will recall from your time in Iraq that there is not much to see except sand and the tracks of jerboa, lizards, and camels. Occasionally camels visit our camp. In the far distance I can see a Bedouin encampment where the camels belong. They come and go on their own, unshepherded.

Intelligence Staff briefing at Headquarters 7th Armoured Brigade, 3 December 1990

[Letter to Jane Watt] *We sometimes hear the World Service talking about the Gulf situation. It seems curious that it is where we happen to be. The Jubayl-Kuwait road groans with military traffic moving north - tanks, guns, the lot. I have never seen such a vast quantity of equipment. If ever there was a signal of intent this is it. The scale of this operation is simply huge. The sheer logistic effort is phenomenal. This is the largest concentration of force ever assembled.*

Tuesday 4 December The sun set dramatically. I was astonished how quickly it disappeared once it had reached the horizon. Timed the disappearance of the sun at the horizon at two minutes and fifteen seconds from the point at which its lower edge touched the horizon to the point at which its upper edge disappeared from view.

Private Graham, Royal Pioneer Corps, Headquarters 7th Armoured Brigade, 3 December 1990

I sleep under the stars. Sometimes a heavy dew forms making everything pretty damp. I get up just before 6 o'clock which is sunrise. Then to breakfast after which I sketch in the relative cool until about 1030. I have to seek cover until about 1500 because it gets too hot. I am not sure what the temperature is but I am gradually becoming acclimatized. I am also getting used to carrying a very heavy load including my art kit and belt order. The latter comprises respirator, NBC kit, water-bottle, and bits and pieces in pouches. It is mandatory to have respirator and NBC kit at hand at all times, and weapon. Lunch at 1200 or so. I then sketch inside, under cover, in the Headquarters using artificial light, or outside, partly shielded by camouflage nets. At about 1500 it starts to cool so I can go out into the open again. At 1700 meal, by which time it is dark. The sunsets are very dramatic. So too are the moonrises. No shortage of sand in this place! No danger of turning up old cigarette ends here as we do on Weymouth beach!

I have made sure I am briefed on the operational and intelligence situation. I also received a brief on 7th Armoured Brigade air assets which are formidable, with the added weight of different types of American fixed-wing aircraft and helicopters. The intelligence situation is very interesting. Suffice to say that with the benefit of satellites there is not a great deal we do not know about the opposition. It seems to be 50/50 at the moment in terms of the political situation and I don't think anyone knows which way it will swing.

Wednesday 5 December Photographed a group of 50-60 camels that had infiltrated the camp. They varied considerably in size, shape, and colour. The range included young camels about half the size of the adults. Some were thin. Others were more heavily built and in better condition. They varied in colour from dark brown to light sand. There was one very large bull that made a rumbling splutter of a call to

Rebroadcast Site Bravo, Nufayl, Saudi Arabia,
5 December 1990

the remainder of the herd. It had an extraordinary pink balloon-like throat pouch that distended during the call, rather like the bullfrogs seen in wildlife films.[10] Met Lance-Corporal Thompson and Lance-Corporal Green of 207 Brigade and Signal Squadron at rebro [rebroadcast] site Bravo.[11] Spent the day sketching the site from two angles. During the hottest part of the day I draped a sheet over myself for shade. Lance-Corporal Green produced an excellent curry, transforming the basic compo [rations] ingredients into something far more palatable. The high ground on which the rebro station was placed commanded an excellent view in every direction. Occasionally I could see a plume of dust as vehicles moved from A to B. I found an ant-hill near the site and saw a small

Corporal Newman, Defence Platoon,
11 Ordnance Company RAOC, Nufayl,
6 December 1990

scorpion which was greenish-yellow in colour.

Returned to Brigade Headquarters at dusk... *Still no mail!! Newspapers come now and then. It is difficult to know what is going on in the world.*

Thursday 6 December Moved to 3 Ordnance Battalion... *I spent the afternoon sketching two sentries in a* sangar [a shallow trench protected with sandbags] *with a machine gun. Then a Warrior gun-barrel being transferred from one 14-ton truck to another.*[12] *I stood in the heat of the day*

Cross-loading a 30mm Rarden cannon, Nufayl, 6 December 1990

balancing my sketch-book on my forearm, as I sketched one of the sentries... I heard something about peace initiatives today. No doubt it will all have changed by the time this letter arrives!

It is a long day. I get up at 5.45, wash my clothes and hang them up on the inside of the camouflage nets. It is then time for breakfast. I am out all day, returning at sunset which lasts for a very short time, then all is black. What a place! I find sketching in the heat of the day very testing but I cover my head with a sheet to make an awning, which works well.

Friday 7 December Remained at 3 Ordnance Battalion.

A JCB of 43 Ordnance Company RAOC loading 155mm artillery
ammunition, Nufayl, 7 December 1990

Saturday 8 December Went to 31 Ordnance Company at the port of Al Jubayl, a 45-minute drive from Battalion Headquarters. *En route* saw many things of interest to use in subsequent sketches. These included: Bedouin tending camels; American cars; water-tanks set on thin stems and shaped like light bulbs hundreds of feet in the air, painted in brilliant colours; the jade sea of the Persian Gulf which is very salty; and a splash of pink on the shoreline which I took to be a flock of flamingos, later confirmed by Captain Tony Crease, Scots DG [Royal Scots Dragoon Guards], a keen amateur ornithologist. Other points I should record are soldiers on relief from the line at Camp 4; the petro-chemical industries that blight the landscape and cluster round the port; lorries, battered and usually overladen; and various plants of the lupin family, convolvulus, and small, rounded, bushy shrubs on thin stems resembling orange trees, which line the main roads converging on the city. Even after only a few days in the desert I was struck by the increase in greenery on the approaches to Jubayl. First the camel-thorn becomes greener and more plentiful; then a few solitary date palms followed by small clusters of palms. Finally serried ranks of trees and thick vegetation that line the main route into the city.

A Challenger Recovery Vehicle cross-loading a Warrior engine, Nufayl, 9 December 1990

Sunday 9 December Spent day at FRG [Forward Repair Group] 7. Returned to Brigade Headquarters after dark but left my camp-bed in a vehicle belonging to FRG 7. Expect an uncomfortable night. I am amazed how many stones lie just beneath the sand surface. In one handful of sand I counted six stones, two very small and four the size of a blackbird egg. Received my first two letters!

Monday 10 December Moved to DS [Dressing Station] One Alpha Royal Army Medical Corps... *On the basis that a few lines are better than nothing a short note because I am on my knees*

Dressing Station One Alpha, Nufayl, 10 December 1990

tonight - literally - scribbling this out by torchlight. Now at the Dressing Station. Very interesting and sobering too. One tenth of British forces in the Gulf are medical staff of one sort or another.[13] *The planning figure for casualties, if it comes to that (which I now doubt, although I thought war a certainty when I left), is expected to be around five per cent, or about 200 a day, in the worst case, for a brigade. I imagine that the chemical threat will add greatly to the difficulties facing medical teams, although they have specially designed de-contaminated tents in which to work. I plan to sketch these tomorrow. Interestingly all medical vehicles here bear the Red Cross with the half moon Red Crescent of the Islamic world alongside. Muslims do not accept the Red Cross because they associate it with the Christian sign of the Cross, which of course it is not... Al Jubayl is full of petro-chemical plants. The largest is ARAMCO (American); the Saudi Petro-Chemical Company (SADAF) is smaller. Profits from oil-based industries have rocketed since the crisis.*[14]

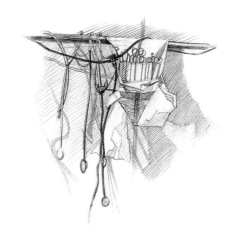

Medical equipment in the Minor Treatment Bay of Dressing Station One Alpha, 11 December 1990

Tuesday 11 December *I am still at Dressing Station 1A. I spent the day drawing the interior of the Treatment Room with its stretchers and medical apparatus. It was a relief to be out of the heat. Sketched some medical instruments hanging from the side of the tent in a wallet, including stethoscopes, tourniquet, and artery forceps. I go to 1 ADTR [1 Armoured Division Transport Regiment] tomorrow. I expect to draw trucks and loads being transferred from A to B... One other good thing from today is that I got some ointment for 'prickly heat' which is affecting my feet badly. It produces madly itchy pink blotches all round the ankle bone. I have ditched my black leather boots in favour of suede desert boots.*

Wednesday 12 December Remained at DS1A.

Thursday 13 December Visited 33 Squadron 1 ADTR commanded by Major Jonathan Lowe, Royal Corps of Transport. Finished sketching at dusk and returned to Regimental Headquarters. Since there was a little light left I decided to visit the camel farm nearby, where I met Muttlaq the owner. He employs a number of workers to tend the animals, including two Pakistani immigrants. I was given tea (*shay*), which was very sweet and served in small glasses with tiny handles. I drank three glasses as it is considered impolite to drink less, but excessive to drink more. Later I was given Arabic coffee (*qahwaah*) from a brass, Turkish-style *dillah*. Arabic coffee tastes nothing like the coffee we know in Europe. It is decidedly aromatic, a thin, green, bitter liquid, flavoured with cardamom seeds. My host was very courteous and dignified. He wore the traditional Arab dress, a *thobe* and a red and white *ghutra*.[15] We discussed camels and confirmed that they vary in colour from dark brown and almost black to light sand, some appearing almost white. We sat round a fire fuelled by the branches and

Camel and camel driver, Nufayl, 16 December 1990

roots of camel-thorn, on two mats laid out on the sand. By this time it was pitch black. The fire crackled, sending sparks leaping into the night. I sat cross-legged for as long as I could. When it became agonizing, I leant sideways against a low padded stool and some heaped rugs in a similar fashion to Muttlaq's cousin, Hussein Abdullah Al Qamadi.

Subjects discussed were these: first the weather; it normally rains in December, which has the effect of packing the loose deep sand, making it much easier to negotiate on foot or by vehicle. It remains 'cool' until July. I took that with a pinch of salt.

Plants: desert flowers, blue, red, and yellow, appear after rain. There are two types of camel-thorn or scrub [possibly *tribulus* and *heliotrope*]. Camels have a decided preference for one or the other, depending on the season of the year. Meat (*lahm*): Arabs eat goat and lamb (*kharoof*) mainly, and sometimes camel. The old animals are tough, but the young ones are tender and taste like veal. The slaughter of a camel is invariably the occasion for a feast and for giving parts of the animal to friends and neighbours. Fish (*samak*): these abound in the Persian Gulf, including shrimps (*gaembaeri*), sea-bream and barracuda (*qidd*).[16] Animals: oryx and gazelle are to be found in the rockier areas of the country to the north.[17] Birds: hawks, particularly peregrine and saker falcons, are highly prized - and priced likewise. Muttlaq was offered a gyrfalcon from Scotland, but declined it on the grounds of cost. A trained hawk can cost more than £10,000.[18] Politics: he was adamant that the Allies should strike now because in his view, Saddam will not withdraw from Kuwait. Dogs: he had two shifty-looking curs that growled and snapped at each other, but both turned out to be friendly.

Friday 14 December Moved to MRG [Medium Repair Group] 7B.

Saturday 15 December Continued sketching at MRG 7B. Later went to the camel farm again where I was given camel's milk in a tin bowl. The milk (*haleeb*) was hot; some dead flies floated on the surface. Then met Hussein Abdullah again,

Camel-thorn, Al Fadhili, late December 1990

'Dogs of the Desert'. Guarding a camel enclosure, Al Fadhili, 18 December 1990

who showed me his *beyt* (tent, literally 'dwelling'). It was spacious, highly decorated in bright colours, with diamond patterns on the side walls. The roof was mainly sage green and maroon, while the floor was carpeted and there were cushions in one corner. Two doorways opened onto an unending view of sand. Then Hussein Abdullah, a Qatari, drove me to see his camels grazing in the desert. Sketched one animal called 'Bahhir Fahal'. Photographed two more called 'G'aud' and 'Khalra Naga', mother and offspring respectively, the latter aged only eight weeks. Then a large bull camel named 'Howwar' or 'Howwara'.[19] Returned to the camel farm where my host was greeted by his two dogs. They ran like the wind alongside the vehicle. One was ginger, the other white with buff-grey blotches, and both had short tails held upright like a German pointer, but were much thinner, smaller, and more rangy. Finally, with reluctance, and on his insistence, I made a sketch of Hussein Abdullah himself, which mercifully was not too bad considering it was baking hot. In my haste I left my sketch-book on the bonnet of the vehicle. We then drove off. Going back later, amazingly, we found it again amidst a maze of vehicle and camel tracks. Hussein Abdullah must have known every inch of that grazing area.

Sunday 16 December Spent the whole morning in a paddock at the camel farm studying and sketching camels. Most of the camels were let out of their enclosure at 0730 as usual, to graze on their own in the desert and return to the camel farm at dusk. A group of about 20 remained in the enclosure including about ten young camels ranging from two weeks to a few days in age. The young camels were very dark in colour, with a woolly coat, and spent much of the time resting on the ground on their knees. The adults ate straw, rested on the ground or drank from the water trough fed by a water tanker, which was backed onto the enclosure and linked by a thick black rubber pipe. I also sketched the enclosure itself with its fodder or straw containers in the centre, surrounded by a chain-link fence on wooden stakes, with a light blue-green windbreak made of old grain bags sewn together. Only managed to draw one camel from an amalgam of different animals as each assumed the side-on pose I had chosen. One camel had the number 652 in Arabic numerals branded on its neck. Then made some sketches of the metal-smiths at MRG 7B.

'Despatch Riders'. Corporal Boyle, 54 Ambulance Support Group, waiting to escort vehicles from Dressing Station One Alpha, 10 December 1990

[Letter to Mrs A E M Watt] *I am immensely impressed by our Army. Everyone is armed to the teeth at all times and I am in no doubt that ours is a very professional Army which an enemy takes on at his peril.*

I have already done 30 pages of sketches. Subjects include the following: sentries, an American group which is part of 7th Armoured Brigade which, in turn, is part of 1 (US) Marine Division,[20] vehicles loading or being loaded, fuel tankers re-fuelling other vehicles, ammunition and stores being cross-loaded from one vehicle to another, despatch riders, the inside and outside of a medical station, engines being lifted into tanks, field kitchens, sunsets and afterglow, recovery vehicles pulling vehicles stuck in sand, a turret being lifted from an infantry vehicle to fix a communication fault, and camels. I am amazed and greatly encouraged by the goodwill and support I have received from officers and soldiers alike at all levels.[21]

I have desert combat kit which is very comfortable and I wear desert boots which are rapidly wearing out. I am hit by tummy bugs every six or seven days, which is a bit debilitating. Water is not a problem and the food is good. At night there is a blackout, which means that the simplest thing, like washing, takes four times longer than normal. I think it is probably quite strenuous organizing oneself, just living, carrying all the paraphernalia required and, in my case, moving from A to B constantly. But what a challenge. Thank Heaven I served my field sketching apprenticeship in fairly severe conditions in Canada and the Falklands.[22] I spent yesterday morning sketching camels in an enclosure. There were 20 camels. Half were young ones ranging in age from two weeks to a matter of days. Woolly-coated chaps with gentle expressions. The adults of course are hideous but quite fascinating to draw.

Monday 17 December Still at MRG 7B. At sunrise sketched two camels. They are incredibly complicated creatures to draw. Then I drew the inside of a Bedouin tent or, more accurately, the interior of the tent belonging to a Pakistani camel driver employed by Muttlaq and Hussein Abdullah.[23] It was very dirty. Nevertheless I had a bowl of camel's milk, which could be disastrous! The man was Mohammad Perwesh who comes from Peshawar. A charming, generous man with a cast in his left eye and full of humour. I also did a sketch of his cooking pots and stove. He was cutting up meat and throwing it into a pot. The sketch of the interior shows a view of the desert stretching away to infinity with the stakes and wind-break of the camel enclosure in the middle distance. An adult camel costs about £1,000 or 7,000 Saudi riyals.[24]

Tuesday 18 December Went down to the camel farm at first light. Sketched 'Tulon', a bull camel. His forelegs were hobbled by a blue rope fastened to a metal stake. He was larger, heavier, and much more muscular than the females. He held his head very high and made deep-throated rumbling calls incessantly while stamping impatiently around his tether. A cantankerous devil.[25] The two Pakistani workers let the camels out of their enclosure at 0730 and the animals moved out in procession into the desert. Occasionally a camel would break into a lolloping canter as the two dogs that guard the camp snapped

A Hydrema light wheeled tractor under repair at 21 Engineer Regiment workshops, Nufayl,
18 December 1990

at their heels. The action of the camels was rather similar to the bucking of cattle when excited or under threat. Thence to 21 Engineer Regiment. Sketched a Hydrema light wheeled tractor under repair. The teeth had sheared off the rack and pinion system.

Wednesday 19 December Roaring toothache most of the day. Extremely hectic with very little sketching done. Went first to 4 Squadron RE [Royal Engineers], commanded by Major Peter Davies. Thence to 45 Squadron RE commanded by Major James Wood. Saw a very long string of camels crossing a road and a flock of goats later, but they were difficult to approach.

Thursday 20 December Sketched a dead jerboa.[26] It was very small, only about four inches long. It was white on its flanks and underside and orange-brown on its back. Returned to 4 Squadron RE. Thence to 1 Field Squadron where I met Captain Bryan Hemmings. Tooth still very sore, so I went to 24 (Airmobile) Field Hospital to see a dentist. Given a small

Sunrise at the leaguer of 1st Battalion, The Staffordshire Regiment, Al Fadhili, 24 December 1990

number of painkillers and a large quantity of penicillin. Sketched a scorpion found by Padre Geoff Sussex in an open sand area at 24 (Airmobile) Field Hospital. Scorpion olive green. Also sketched a much smaller scorpion in an attack profile.

Friday 21 December Tooth agonizing. Moved from 21 Engineer Regiment to 1 Staffords [1st Battalion, The Staffordshire Regiment]. Battalion concentrated in order to celebrate Ferozeshah Day. This action was fought in 1845 in the Punjab during the First Sikh War, and is the Regiment's principal battle honour.

Saturday 22 December Drew a profile of the tent of the Commanding Officer 1 Staffords, set against a background of the rising sun. Very cold; had three jerseys on. The sun came up amazingly quickly. Thence to C Company, commanded by Major John Rochelle. The company were having a maintenance day, which meant I had a clear view of the vehicles without camouflage nets. Spent most of the day with 9 Platoon, commanded by Sergeant Walker. The inside of rear door of the APC [Armoured Personnel Carrier] bore the words 'Merry Christmas', set amongst a sea of Christmas cards and a Christmas stocking. At one point the platoon mail-bag arrived. Sergeant Walker, kneeling on the sand, distributed the mail to the half-circle of soldiers who had gathered to collect post for their respective crews. I made some careful studies of the Warrior APC which I had not examined before at close quarters. Drew quick sketches of a Warrior gunner seen from the back deck with a Staffords' pennant unfurled on the vehicle antenna, another Warrior beyond and a few more on the move, throwing up billowing clouds of sand. Tooth so painful I went to 33 Field Hospital at Jubayl. The tooth was badly inflamed and the filling was replaced. Once again it is as sore as ever but I hope it will now subside. Thank Heaven for Panadol! The benefits were a meal and a shower at Camp 4 and a new pair of desert boots.

Sunday 23 December My tooth has at last quietened down. Remained at 1 Staffords.

Monday 24 December Spent the day at the 'White Farm' [a group of whitewashed buildings], where the men of 1 Staffords leaguered for 18 days. Sketched the farm from the Staffords' sentry post, with some camel tracks leading

Desert mosque and minaret, Al Fadhili,
24 December 1990

into the picture. Then sketched a desert mosque and various details of the building, including the minaret, at the top of which was the crescent-moon of Islam in weathered copper.[27] Moved to the centre of the camel farm to sketch an Arab cross-bred mare called 'Shafi' (wheat). A sadly neglected animal.[28] I doubt if she ever leaves her small compound surrounded by its chain-link fence. Late in the afternoon a group of camels came up to the compound. They towered above the mare but exchanged nuzzles through the wire. I finally completed a head study of a donkey, having first made separate studies of its ear, eye and nostril. A well-educated Bangladeshi, Sheikh Oliur Rahman Babor, showed me round and explained how the farm was run. I saw fat-tailed sheep and goats resting on straw and sheltering from the baking heat under a low roof of timber and corrugated iron. In a separate enclosure were four camels with skin complaints, which were being treated with some form of disinfectant.

Tuesday 25 December Moved to the QRIH [Queen's Royal Irish Hussars] after three days with 1 Staffords. Spent an excellent Christmas Day as a guest of the Commanding Officer, Colonel Arthur Denaro. The Regiment gathered around midday, in a scene strongly reminiscent of British soldiers in the Western Desert during the Second World War. A motley-looking band, dressed in a variety of head-gear, including *shamaghs* [Arab head-dress],[29] the Irish Hussars' dark green tent hats braided with gold, cotton camouflage bush hats, and the service dress hats of officers of 17/21L [17th/21st Lancers].[30] Lunch began with a plastic mug full of prawns, followed by turkey, roast potatoes and Brussels sprouts; then Christmas pudding and custard. There was alcohol-free beer and low-alcohol wine. The men stood around in groups, some resting plates and cups on the bonnets of Land Rovers with the wind and driven sand gusting through the encampment, obscuring groups of figures in the middle and far distance at times. I made a small sketch of a group of 17/21L holding a makeshift lance and pennant. The pennant was scarlet and white, commemorating British victories over Napoleon's Polish Lancers. Lieutenant-General Sir Peter de la Billière, the supremely modest Commander British Forces Middle East, moved quietly among the throng, but always noticed. In the evening the Regiment staged a revue with the Regimental band present. Again reminiscent of former wartime scenes, with music and laughter wafting across the desert and hundreds of darkened figures surrounding a makeshift stage with footlights. Soldiers were packed into an amphitheatre formed by 4-ton trucks parked in a semicircle, either seated, standing, or packed tightly in rows inside the vehicles with the side gates lowered and side canopies removed. Some were perched in or on the cab, while others found vantage points on the canvas roof canopies. After the National Anthem, groups of men drifted away into the night. I went back to the Headquarters and spent a few moments round a six-foot table, eating Stilton cheese and ginger cake, washed down with black coffee and alcohol-free beer. Then the group, consisting of Colonel Arthur Denaro; the Second-in-Command, Major Mark O'Reilly; and the Adjutant, Captain Andrew Cuthbert, made their way back to their respective vehicles.

I recall snippets of conversation that day which had to do with a different world: fishing the Thurso, skiing in France, polo, and racing. There was grouse paté and French paté, biscuits from Harrods, and hampers from Fortnum and Mason, packed with black olives, anchovies, smoked oysters and crystallized fruit. Zero Hotel (the Officers' Mess) consisted of a tent with a fridge and fan in one corner, with rows of Christmas cards hanging on strings and a small Christmas tree in a box. Earlier in the day we visited the ANGLICO [US Marine Corps Air and Naval Gunfire Liaison Company] contingent.[31] They were immensely hospitable and had a small table groaning with liver sausage and endless varieties of cakes and 'cookies' sent from the homeland. The US Marines' motto is 'Thunder from the sea; lightning from the sky'. The irreverent British retort was 'and biscuits from a tin', which our Allies took in good heart. They are a generous and open people.

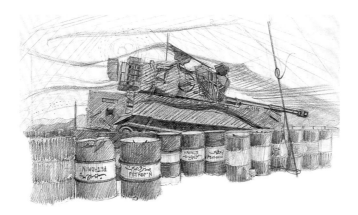

An M109 self-propelled howitzer of 137 (Java) Battery RA
under camouflage nets, 26 December 1990

Wednesday 26 December Moved to 40 Field Regiment Royal Artillery. Went to 137 (Java) Battery, commanded by Major Simon Lloyd. Sketched an M109 [self-propelled howitzer] under a camouflage net in a gun position surrounded by oil barrels filled with sand.[32] The name of Java Battery dates from 1811 when there was a struggle between France and Britain for control of that island.

Thursday 27 December Met Major Chris Nelson, the commander of 10 (Assaye) Air Defence Battery [Royal Artillery]. Normally, their task is protection of routes and vulnerable points. In the desert their main task is to protect tanks. The battery is named 'Assaye' after the battle fought by Wellington against the Marathas in India in 1803. Thence to 129 (Dragon) Battery. This battery's title commemorates the battle of Chin-kiang-foo, fought during the First China War in 1842. Sketched a bitch puppy called 'Bert', adopted by an M109 crew.

Friday 28 December Moved to 38 Battery, which was formed originally in 1768 as the 4th Company of the Bombay Artillery. In 1799 it first saw action at Seringapatam against Tipu Sultan of Mysore. The battery then adopted Tipu's Bengal tiger emblem. Climbed into NBC kit because Iraq had fired another Scud rocket. Then returned to Camp 4. Had a hot shower for the first time in a month. Bliss! Slept badly. Too comfortable!

Saturday 29 December Wrote letters and washed desert combats three times. Almost as dirty after the third wash, so I gave up. Will have to do! Collected from Camp 4 by Padre Philip Majcher in a Toyota 'Land Cruiser'. Scores of these vehicles have been loaned to the British Army by the Saudi government. Moved to Scots DG. Sketched a camel at the White Farm *en route* with some black Bedouin tents in the background. The Bedouin women wore black cloaks.[33]

Lance-Corporal Henderson,
Royal Scots Dragoon Guards, on sentry duty at St Andrews Camp, Nufayl, 30 December 1990

Sunday 30 December Extremely cold night. I do not have enough cold weather kit and now have a raging cold. Extraordinary for Saudi Arabia! My respirator does not fit properly. It leaks under my chin on the right side. I will get another one tomorrow. Sketched the dawn. Then a sentry post at St Andrews Camp, which is a training and rest camp for the Royal Scots Dragoon Guards. I then photographed and sketched an informal Communion service taken by Padre Majcher. Returned to Regimental Headquarters where I am sharing a bivvy [bivouac] with Padre Majcher. At supper, a camel came into the tent and began eating from one of the metal food containers. The camel ate a complete loaf of bread with its wrapper and about ten apples. It also drank from a bucket, slurping loudly, and later devoured part of the camouflage net which, presumably, it took for leaves, all against the backdrop of a spectacular sunset, or more accurately, its afterglow. I recall that after breakfast the same day, the same animal chewed an empty compo tin for at least three minutes before spitting it out. The tin was crushed flat.

'White Heat'. Royal Scots Dragoon Guards Challenger tanks being loaded onto transporters,
31 December 1990

Monday 31 December Moved 70 kilometres north with Scots DG from Al Fadhili to Abu Hadriyah near the coastal area of Ras Az Zawr. Began the day at a point known as the 'petrol station' - a single pump in the middle of nowhere, except for a water truck, a few ramshackle shanties, and a bull camel in a dusty compound surrounded by a chain-link fence. The animal was on the move almost constantly, making it extremely difficult to draw. Its forelegs were hobbled and it had large, hardened patches of skin on the knees of its forelegs and on the upper thighs of its hind legs. Sparrows and wagtails flew in and out of the pen, picking up grain.

Challenger tanks were being loaded onto tank transporters.[34] The transporters arrived first, using a dusty track and turning in a wide sweep at the 'petrol station'. They then retraced their approach route, heading for the Jubayl-Kuwait road, halted in a long line and prepared to receive the tanks. The tanks headed toward them across the desert with white dust, black diesel exhaust, and particles of orange sand rising in a thick cloud and obscuring the columns as they thundered forward to the loading point. It was baking hot. I then travelled to Jubayl with the Padre to 33 Field Hospital where he visited two soldiers burnt in a petrol cooker blaze. While at Camp 4 I telephoned Jane [my wife] but she was out. Photographed several plants with brightly coloured flowers. Returned to the desert at dusk, finally arriving at the new regimental leaguer at Saihad Murair or Abu Hadriyah, near Devil Dog Dragoon Range.[35] Spent New Year's Eve with the Padre, camouflaging a vehicle, then digging a trench and filling sandbags. Major Mark Auchinleck gave me a swig of whisky from his water-bottle to bring in the New Year - but early, about 2130. Got to bed at 2330, totally exhausted.

Tuesday 1 January 1991 Reveille at 0530 with 'stand to' from 0545 to 0615. Sketched the dawn with coloured pencils. Made a pencil sketch of RSM [Regimental Sergeant-Major] 'Jock' Allan digging a trench, entitled 'smoke break'. Walked to Devil Dog Dragoon Range where I sketched Lance-Corporal Wood of 3rd Troop D Squadron reading an Edinburgh daily newspaper on top of a Challenger. The Squadron had just completed its pre-firing checks for the following day. As I returned to RHQ [Regimental Headquarters] I noticed tiny cone-shaped sea shells lying on the surface of the ground in places. Finally, sketched an FV434 [tracked maintenance vehicle] replacing an APU [Auxiliary Power Unit] in the Brigade Commander's Challenger. Some general points: this area is much harder under foot. There are innumerable snake-holes, but snakes and scorpions are in winter hibernation now. It is not advisable to sleep too close to the cam[ouflage] net where it joins the ground because scorpions can climb quite well. Also, washing water should not be thrown away near tents because water attracts snakes and most snakes here are dangerous.[36] There are countless seeds from camel-thorn mixed with the sand in this part of the desert. They are about the size of a thumb-nail and very painful to tread on - extremely nasty.

Challengers of the Royal Scots Dragoon Guards firing on Devil Dog Dragoon Range, Abu Hadriyah, 2 January 1991

Wednesday 2 January Spent the whole day at Devil Dog Dragoon Range, watching D Squadron and A Squadron Scots DG practise firing. Concentrated on crews resting, preparing their tanks, firing, and tanks moving off the firing point. Made some careful studies of the flash at the moment of firing, and studies of the different dust and engine exhaust patterns of a Challenger moving slowly and flat out.

Thursday 3 January Spent the whole day on the range watching B Squadron shooting. Observed muzzle flashes closely and drew a tank with a traverse gearbox problem being attended by REME [Royal Electrical and Mechanical Engineers]... *This is no picnic. There is a howling wind tonight and it is really cold. I have got four layers on. I have a bad cough. I find life physically strenuous. I have been on the move for a month now, re-packing my kit every three days. The day starts at 0530. We get up, don helmets, gather NBC kit, respirators, and weapons, and climb into trenches. 'Stand to' is from 0545 to 0615.*

New Year's Eve found us on the move again and setting up in a new place. I spent New Year's Eve with the Scots DG Padre, digging a trench. The Second-in-Command, Mark Auchinleck, came round during our 'dig' and gave me a swig of whisky from his water-bottle. I fell into my pit pretty tired. I am now in the Battle Group Headquarters writing this letter.[37] It is crowded and there is very little light... Spent the past few days drawing tanks firing on a range carved out of the desert. Pretty dramatic with tanks performing excellently.

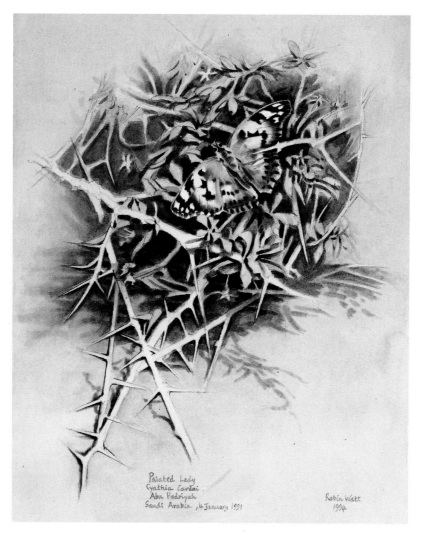

A Painted Lady butterfly resting on camel-thorn, Abu Hadriyah,
4 January 1991

Friday 4 January Sketched the only butterfly I have seen so far. Red and orange with black spots, but not a Red Admiral![38] The insect sunned itself on the sand and then alighted on some camel-thorn nearby. The latter had small delicate violet trumpet-shaped flowers that contrasted with the fearsome thorns of the plant and the red-orange of the butterfly. Then moved by Land Rover to the Irish Hussars east of Abu Hadriyah. There sketched a command troop tank, commanded by Cornet James Moseley. The tank was decammed [decamouflaged] and the crew were doing gun checks.

[Letter to Mrs A E M Watt] *The Queen's Royal Irish Hussars have taken me under their wing. The Regiment is the nearest thing to a family I have seen, and the sense of family is heightened by the circumstances... I am not sure how things are going to work out or when. All I can say is that I believe in our leadership and in General Sir Peter de la Billière in particular. I am quite certain he will ensure that casualties are minimized. I am also certain that air power is the key. I hope there are no Iraqis there when the Allies move into Kuwait!*

Saturday 5 January 'Stand to' at first light with command troop. Then preparation by the Irish Hussars for exercise HOUBARA RAT.[39] The aim of the exercise is to practise a dry and live-firing offensive operation. My intention is to follow this exercise through from start to finish. The exercise will involve moving to a Concentration Area at first light and then mounting a battle group attack on two objectives. Attended a Regimental Orders Group and a briefing which outlined the likely role and tasks of the Regiment in the event of war. The broad mechanics of the operation were explained with the use of a model in the sand roped off by orange tape with a cam[ouflage] pole at each corner. The models representing tank troops were made of black masking tape and cardboard, with call signs superimposed in felt pen. Sore arm - had two BW [Biological Warfare] injections.

A Challenger of The Queen's Royal Irish Hussars training at Abu Hadriyah, 8 January 1991

Sunday 6/Monday 7 January The day began at 0345. Joined Sergeant Moore REME on an FV434 and moved to the Assembly Area by first light where we cammed up [camouflaged] the vehicle and dug a shelter trench. Exercise HOUBARA RAT involved two battle group attacks, the first by day, the second by night. Both attacks went very well and were finished by the early hours of the following morning. Then began a long night march from the range to our original start-point which took the rest of the night. It was bitterly cold. Got in at 0430. 'Stand to' was one hour later. Felt ghastly, but now adept at putting up and taking down cam nets and digging shelter trenches in the dark. Main recollections were the bitter cold of a desert night, the thud of artillery and the thunder of armour on the move. The following day [Monday 7 January] moved in a tracked armoured personnel carrier to a new area with the Irish Hussars Battle Group. Made several sketches but too tired to concentrate.

It's been difficult keeping in touch because of moving and the fact that it gets dark at 1745. Consequently, when I have finished my round of sketching, it is time for 'stand to' again and once it is dark we cannot use light. Now sitting in my NBC kit in an APC, trying to sketch a field firing exercise for QRIH. It is their last exercise before January 15 [the deadline of the Allied ultimatum to Iraq]. Aeroplanes, tanks, artillery, the lot. Had two BW jabs yesterday. Jolly painful!

Tuesday 8 January Spent most of the day trying to establish atmosphere, that is dust thrown up by moving tanks at different speeds or by the blast caused by tanks firing; and exhaust fumes from the APU or 'Aux Jenny' and main engines. Noted the blue smoke from the APU and the black smoke from the main engine. Also heavy dust particles thrown up by the tracks of moving tanks and the lighter, smaller particles that lifted and then hung in the atmosphere mingling with blue-violet sky, both being the same tone. Made detailed observations of six tanks and their crews as follows: Corporal Jonas of *Donaghadee* bore-sighting,[40] Trooper Winn loading bag-charges onto *Ballyjamesduff*, Corporal Rouayne moving away from a replenishment point on *Blackrock*, and Sergeant Connor catching boxes of rations and Coca-Cola cans being thrown up onto the turret of *Belcoo*. I also noted Lieutenant Tim Buxton loading rations onto *Ballycastle* and Sergeant Griffin re-fuelling *Belleek*.

Wednesday 9 January One sketch of the dawn. Sketched tanks firing during the day. Two colour sketches at dusk from a trench at 'stand to'.

'Nerium Oleander'. Camp 4, Al Jubayl, Saudi Arabia, 30 December 1990

Thursday 10 January Went to Brigade Headquarters to find out if I am to stay in the Gulf or not. Meanwhile the Irish Hussars have taken me under their wing... *The current arrangement is that I should return to England on 14th January but the Commander 7th Armoured Brigade, Brigadier Cordingley, has written a letter asking for me to remain here. By the time this letter arrives I shall know whether I stay or not.*

[Letter to Mrs A E M Watt] *I have drawn all sorts of things: camels, donkeys, a horse (a small cross-breed), a puppy, a jerboa, a scorpion, and guns, tanks, soldiers, sunsets and sunrises, even a butterfly and a wagtail... I spoke to Major Mark Auchinleck, Second-in-Command Scots DG, who is interested in plants. He has identified the following plants at Camp 4 in Jubayl: bougainvillaea, oleander, eucalyptus, callistemon (bottle brush tree), hibiscus and lantana... It's freezing at night now. Also very windy. This is the season of sandstorms. Also the* sabhkhats *or* salt marshes, *which are dry in summer, are filling up as the water table rises. We have had a little rain. Am used to getting up at 0515 for 'stand to' ie full kit, weapon and helmet, then climbing into a trench for 30 minutes. The same process*

An infantryman of 1st Battalion, The Staffordshire Regiment, training at
Al Fadhili, late December 1990

takes place at last light. A time for quiet reflection and getting perishing cold!! Food very good. Am eating like a horse. We all wear shamaghs *for warmth... I shall remain with Arthur Denaro and the QRIH who are the best group of men one could possibly be with. Arthur himself is ex-Oman and an exceptional leader. His men think the world of him... I arrived at The Queen's Royal Irish Hussars for a live firing exercise with tanks, artillery, the lot. Safety margins were cut to the minimum. The Staffords, running a similar exercise, suffered some casualties: the Commanding Officer, the Second-in-Command, and the RSM all received grenade splinters, but they are all fit and well now! Incidentally the Staffords are a very good tough lot. The political situation of course does not look good and we expect to go to war.*

Friday 11 January Moved to Camp 4 to re-organize my kit for the last time. Telephoned my mother and my wife. The mail system has gone haywire. It seems more likely by the hour that we will go to war. Spent the day having a tooth fixed; buying film, a toothbrush, a razor; sewing buttons onto trousers; and repairing a ripped back pocket. Washed clothes, wrote diary. Made list of things to do the following day. Received a parcel with art supplies.

Saturday 12 January Spent most of the day sorting out equipment. Found time to sketch six different flowers and photograph two species of butterfly. The first looked rather similar to a dull version of a Red Admiral. The other had strong vibrant colours with clearly defined markings. The overall colour was an orange-russet veering to deep chestnut with dabs of black and white.[41] *I must say we are all feeling rather sombre about life. No one is 'up and at them', just very professional and rather quiet.*

Sunday 13 January Moved into the field from Camp 4, two hours' journey by road. The umbilical cord with Camp 4 has been finally cut. A very wet night. It rained without pause. Thick glutinous mud turned the desert surface into a skating rink, particularly in the shallow bowls in the desert known as *sabhkhats*. God knows where my mail has gone. Meanwhile January 15 looms and with it the possibility of a pre-emptive attack by Iraq. War now seems a certainty. The hope is that the Allied air strike will break Iraq's will to resist. I hope to go into action to make observations at first hand with Scots DG, QRIH or 1 Staffords.

We have been told there is no roulement [troop replacements]. *All those 'in theatre' will remain until the operation is finished. Most think this will mean April/May at latest. Thank you for putting up with all this. I am sure we will say in retrospect that we have learnt many things that others may never learn. I find destruction depressing although curiously the havoc we must bring to bear will act as our best defence. I am sitting in a vehicle. It is grey and overcast, and it has been raining all day and most of the night too. The sand has turned to glutinous mud.*

Equipment is a nightmare. The less the better really. No wonder it's called impedimenta *in the Latin books at school. I can think of a few more names for it!! But am now firmly established with QRIH. That means that I can dump part of my equipment when required. As it is we travel heavy, the minimum being helmet, weapon, full webbing, and NBC kit. Have taken ages to write this letter. We are waiting for Arthur Denaro to be briefed by the General. Then we go back to the QRIH leaguer.*

I am with an amazingly good bunch of people. I have never known such comradeship since I have been in the Army except, briefly, during 'P' Company [the selection course for the Royal Armoured Corps Parachute Squadron] *20 years ago. People one has met only once, possibly weeks before, come up and shake one by the hand like long-lost friends.*

Monday 14 January It poured with rain all night. Rain got into the tent and those without waterproof clothing were soaked. I immediately sent for my Gore-tex which will be useful to keep the wind off at night even if the rain has stopped by the time I receive it. I sincerely hope it has, because life will become pretty uncomfortable otherwise. Spent the day cleaning my weapon, checking magazines, digging water channels round the tent, and reading up the intelligence picture of Iraqi forces. By the evening the wind was still buffeting the tents. Report that Iraqi Special Forces crossed the border overnight. Sentries were doubled.

I saw Brigadier Patrick Cordingley before I left Jubayl where he happened to be just for the day. He said it was important to record events. I am trying like hell!... It is cold, wet, and pretty nasty and nobody's done anything yet! It is 8 o'clock in the evening. We 'stand to' in our trenches at last light. Most people are in bed by 7.30 or 8 because we are up just after 5 for the morning 'stand to'.

It is interesting to see commanders doing the things they normally do in training but this time with real conviction; and to see them tackling those subjects that they are not normally called upon to emphasize, such as coping with fear, reaction to enemy fire, comradeship, the importance of religion, the role of the Padre, battle stress. These are difficult areas, because they often go beyond the personal experience of many commanders. There are also the more tangible subjects such as the finer aspects of NBC, casevac [casualty evacuation] *and first aid (for example, how to put in an IV* [intravenous drip] *or fit an airway). The care and thoroughness with which these subjects are addressed is impressive.*

There is an Orders Group every morning. It always begins with the Lord's Prayer. We also had a service the other day, which itself fosters comradeship and a common sense of purpose. I ought to go to bed now. About 9.30. The wind is still beating about. I must get over to the Headquarters vehicles to post this letter, then find my way back to my own shelter.

Tuesday 15 January Training day which began with briefings by the Intelligence Officer, Captain Tom Beckett, and the Operations Officer, Captain Robert Hutton. The Intelligence Officer described the Iraqi obstacle belt which appeared formidable. It was believed to consist of six lines of defence, including a flame-trench filled with oil ready for ignition, a minefield, a wire entanglement, and a wire fence, which are covered by infantry dug-in, and an armoured counter-attack force.

The Operations Officer described the plan for the move of 1st (BR) Division 340 kilometres to the north-west with words to this effect;

> 'The move will take place from 17-21 January using 'Route Dodge' [the Oil Tapline Road].[42] There are three phases and a preliminary phase involving recce and preparation. Phase 1 is a controlled move to a Concentration Area via a Release Point. In Phase 2 we continue training and liaise with flanks. Phase 3 will be subsequent operations. The layout on the ground in the new Concentration Area will be QRIH forward right, Scots DG forward left and 1 Staffords rear. The area is very flat. The going is hard and covered with stones. The FMA [Force Maintenance Area] is protected by Hawk, Rapier, Javelin and Patriot [surface-to-air missiles, or SAMs].

Then Major Mark O'Reilly, the Second-in-Command, described Route Dodge as follows;
> 'Route Dodge is chaos with soldiers up to their knees in mud. It is the equivalent of a B vehicle route with one lane. There are six different nations on the move complicated by breakdowns, accidents, and refugees. Frequent diversions sometimes make it difficult to tell if one is on the correct route or not. There is a need for great patience. There is fear in the air, with immigrants going for their lives. In summary, the route is fascinating but chaos.

Next, Colonel Arthur Denaro had this to say on the move to the Concentration Area;
> 'We are part of VII Corps which is four times the size of 1st (BR) Division. Seeing a Corps going to war is a spectacle that defies description. To the north is an Egyptian Division, to the north-west a Saudi Division, to the west a Syrian Division, to the south 1 (US) Armoured Cavalry Regiment, which is itself the size of a British Division, and to the south-east is 1 (US) Infantry Division. We must continue our normal training and preparation when we get there. We will still be 80 kilometres from the border, but we must expect a reactive strike south or defections by the Iraqis. We need to continue to get the detail right. There will be a Divisional practice move. There will also be a Divisional FTX [Field Training Exercise] to rehearse our move through the US Division.

The training day ended with comments by the Regimental Padre, the Battle Group Commander and the Brigade Commander with words to this effect;

Father Sean Scanlon,
> 'The basic thing to remember is that this is a 'just war'. Already we see in ourselves signs of anxiety. We must prepare ourselves for sights we have never seen. As soldiers we must be ruthless in the application of force, but it is of paramount importance that we never lose respect for human life. We must have respect for the Iraqi dead, for if we lose that, we lose respect for ourselves. There is no honour in victory, only in how victory is achieved.

Brigadier P A J Cordingley,
> 'We see the inevitability of war, but it is not inevitable that we will be committed or even cross the Start Line. The pressure is on wives and families rather than ourselves because of the comradeship we share. Do not become over-confident. Do not be incautious. Remember the importance of fire and movement.

Colonel Arthur Denaro,
> 'Three points: the importance of operational security, the care of your men, and the determination to reach the objective despite possible casualties.

The deadline ran out today at 0800. The main fear is that this maniac will launch a pre-emptive attack. We are not sure when the air war will start, but you will be well informed when it does, and the effects should be devastating. There is a great deal of confidence in this and when launched, targets will be sought out by the greatest concentration of aircraft ever assembled in the history of warfare. This will afford our best protection. More than that I should not say except that we remain under command 1 (US) Marine Division, itself part of 1 (US) Marine Corps.[43] Having said that I don't mind what element of the US Army I am under, because their firepower is so massive it really doesn't make much difference!

For once I am writing this in daylight. The weather is better today and we have some sun. We spent three miserable days with lashing rain and wind. We all hope this phase is now over, but it could return. Please send a mirror, a washing bag and, most important of all, my Gore-tex jacket.

1   Saudi Arabia emerged as a country in 1932 under Abdul Aziz Ibn Saud, created by the union of the Nejd, Hijaz, Asir and Al Hasa regions. It was Ibn Saud's stunningly successful ability to transform the wasteful tribal feuding into a potent political weapon that finally made unity possible. But victory was hard won. Apart from some abandoned gold mines and the pearls of the Gulf, the economy of Saudi Arabia continued to depend on the date palm and camels up to the late 1930s and it remained a harsh land dominated by feuding Bedouin. Oil was struck at Jabal Dhahran in 1938, and since that time the House of Saud has become one of the most influential ruling families in the world. Saudi Arabia is an Arab Kingdom, won by Arabs and ruled over by Arabs of the purest stock. It is this quality of national identity that gives the state its authority and prestige, backed by the immense wealth of oil revenues.

2   Al Jubayl in Saudi Arabia was the point of disembarkation for British ground forces in the Gulf. Situated on the coast, some 150 miles from the border with Kuwait, it began as a fishing village and is now a major industrial city with oil refineries, petro-chemical plants, fertilizer plants, a steel mill, and a desalination plant that pipes fresh water as far as the capital, Riyadh.

3   Camp 4 was previously a non-European oil workers' compound. It had been taken over by 7th Armoured Brigade as a training and fitness centre and to give soldiers a break from the desert.

4   Sea convolvulus, or *Calystegia soldanella*, a trailing perennial which thrives in saline conditions.

5   Over 80 Scud missiles were fired by Iraq during the Gulf war, against targets in Israel and Saudi Arabia. However, the attempt to increase Arab support for Iraq by drawing Israel into the war was a failure. Although many Scuds were intercepted by American 'Patriot' missiles or fell harmlessly in remote areas, several caused extensive Israeli civilian casualties. Another notable target was a United States barracks near Dhahran, struck on 26 February 1991 with over 100 casualties. Although all the Scuds actually fired were fitted with conventional high explosive warheads, they were presumed capable of delivering chemical and biological weapons, and the destruction of Scud launching sites was therefore a high priority for the Allies. By the end of the war, the Scud threat had been greatly reduced by Allied air strikes and the operations of British and American Special Forces.

6   Iraq and Saudi Arabia are the world's leading producers and exporters of dates. Dates have always been a staple food in Arabia, and the date palm or *Phoenix dactylifera* has been grown there for 4,000 years. It needs less water than any other food crop, can tolerate a high level of salinity, and can bear fruit for two centuries. The palm grows to a height of 100 feet, reaches maturity at 12 years, and can produce up to 200 kilos of dates annually. The trunk of the tree provides timber for building houses, boats, fences, and

fish traps. The fronds and leaves are used to make brooms, rope, mats, and baskets, and the leaf bases and fruit stalks provide fuel. The fruit itself is used to make vinegar, sweet pickle, and chutney; flavouring for oranges, bananas, and almonds; and the Bedouin dish *canua*. The crushed stones are fed to cattle. The terminal buds are used in vegetable salads and even the shade protects crops. It is not surprising that the date palm is emblazoned on the national emblem of Saudi Arabia.

7   The low bushes were *Lantana camara*, a shrub of the vervain family introduced from tropical America. It has numerous yellow, orange, red, lavender or white flowers in dense clusters and can grow to twenty feet in the tropics.

8   The desert vegetation appears uniform but varies greatly. Camel -thorn, *tribulus* (or *zahra*, meaning 'The Flower' in Arabic) provides the best grazing for camels. It is almost as revered by the desert tribes as the date palm and they are reluctant to burn it. Heliotrope or *rimran* grows on hard sand in hollows. Like *tribulus* its brittle silver branches often appear dead but both plants have long trailing roots reaching down to the water table. Other desert plants include the sedge *qassis*; a straggling bush with fragile branches, *abal*, which is also good grazing for camels; and *harm*, a bright green salt bush.

9   It must have taken many months to build the network of trenches along the 260-mile length of Kuwait's border that were filled with oil to impede the Allied advance. It appears that, like so many ideas conceived by the Iraqi leadership, the plan had a fatal flaw. When the Allied attack came the heavy crude oil failed to ignite.

10   The camel's 'throat pouch' is an air sac which, when fully inflated, overhangs the animal's lower jaw. The air sac then deflates and disappears into its throat with a gurgling sound. Bull camels can be dangerous. There is one account of a bull killing a man and his son as they sat round a fire at night and then biting off the kneecap of another man who attempted to rescue them.

11   A signal station used to boost ground communication signals.

12   Warrior is a mechanized combat vehicle, in service with the British Army since 1987. It is used principally as an infantry fighting vehicle, carrying a crew of three and a further seven infantrymen.

13   Over 5,000 British medical personnel were eventually deployed in the Gulf. The very high level of medical support required a call-out of a significant number of Reservists for the first time since the Suez Crisis of 1956.

14   We were in the Eastern Province of Saudi Arabia, which is now dominated by the oil

towns clustered around Dhahran. The city was built by Italian prisoners of war from Abyssinia and Eritrea, and by imported Indian and Iraqi labour. An industrial area 50 miles long now extends northwards along the coast of the Persian Gulf from Dhahran to Al Jubayl, and the oil company ARAMCO is based at Dhahran. Originally an Arabian-American company formed in 1944 to supply American operations against the Japanese in the Pacific, ARAMCO is now Saudi-controlled. Saudi Arabia is the world's largest producer of oil and the country has 25 per cent of the World's oil reserves.

15   One of the distinguishing characteristics of Saudi society is the apparent uniformity of dress, itself a sign of equality in the eyes of Allah. A Saudi almost invariably wears the white *thobe*, a full length shirt-like garment made of white cotton, or silk in the case of a king. In winter a heavier material is used and the *thobe* may be dark or striped. The traditional outer robe or cloak, known as a *mislah*, is black, brown or cream and trimmed with gold thread. His headdress consists of a skull cap over which is placed the *ghutra*, a triangular folded cloth with a red and white check, sometimes changing to a plain white headdress of finer material in hot weather. It is held in place by a double corded *ageyl* made of black wool which the Bedouin traditionally used to hobble their camels. Close observation of an Arab's dress, for instance the tilt or disposition of his *ageyl*, can reveal his place of origin.

16   Eighty per cent of Saudi Arabia's fishing catch is destined for home consumption. However, top quality shrimps are exported, mainly to the United States and Japan.

17   The oryx, a large antelope once plentiful in Arabia, has become almost extinct with the use of modern rifles and wheeled transport. Fortunately a fine herd is being reared in captivity in Qatar.

18   Saker and peregrine falcons are the favourite birds of prey used by falconers in Saudi Arabia. Sakers, *Falco sacer*, known as *hurr* in Arabic, live in the steppes of central Asia and are migrants to North Africa and the Middle East. Their principal quarry is the houbara or McQueen's bustard, and the desert hare. The peregrine, known as *shahin* in Arabic, is probably the most highly esteemed bird of prey in falconry circles, famous for its beauty and speed in flight. It can reach speeds of 90 miles per hour when diving or 'stooping' on its prey. The female of the species is larger than the male; the latter is known as a tiercel. The gyrfalcon, *Falco rusticolus*, is the fastest and largest longwing in the world and originates in the Arctic. It is much sought by falconers, particularly the pure white variety, mainly for its prestige value and majestic appearance, but in performance it cannot match the peregrine or the saker. The Arabs claim to be able to train a wild falcon in as little as fifteen days, partly because the falconer is never separated from his charge. An Arab training a bird carries it everywhere with him and even sleeps with it perched on a block by his head. During the day he strokes it and speaks to it, hooding and unhooding it constantly.

19   *Bahhir Fahal* means 'dazzling star', *G'aud* is a young camel, *Khalra Naga* means the best offspring or the pick of the field, *naga* female camel, and *howwar* a yearling male camel. I was told that if an old camel weakens and falls in its tracks it is doused in petrol and set on fire but for some unknown reason without killing it first. Burial would be too difficult and take too long. Furthermore a buried corpse is likely to be investigated by dung beetles. Flies then reach the carcass via the tunnels created by the beetles, thus aggravating the fly problem. Water could be so scarce that it was sometimes impossible to let a camel drink. Instead, water was poured up its nostrils from a kettle to keep it alive just long enough to reach the next oasis.

20   When 7th Armoured Brigade arrived in Saudi Arabia in October 1990, it was placed under the tactical control of 1 (US) Marine Division. In January 1991, as part of the Allied deception plan, the British ground forces, now 1st (BR) Armoured Division, were moved west and transferred to the tactical control of VII (US) Corps.

21   I would have given much for the opportunity to record more, not only of the activities of British soldiers in the desert but also of Arabia, the Bedouin in particular. In his book *Arabian Sands*, Wilfred Thesiger observed of those who may attempt to study Arabia and its people in the future, 'they (the visitors) will move about in cars and keep in touch with the outside world by wireless. They will bring back results far more interesting than mine, but they will never know the spirit of the land, nor the greatness of the Arabs'. He also made this observation of the Bedouin, 'I shall always remember how often I was humbled by those illiterate herdsmen who possessed in so much greater measure than I, generosity, courage, endurance, patience and lighthearted gallantry. Among no other people have I felt the same sense of personal inferiority.' The humble words of a great and distinguished traveller who won a DSO in the Western Desert with the SAS in 1941, and was appointed CBE in 1968.

22   In 1986-88, the artist completed a two-year exchange posting as an instructor at the Combined Arms Training Centre, Gagetown, New Brunswick, Canada. In 1989 he served for six months as a Civil-Military Liaison Officer in the Falkland Islands.

23   Saudi Arabia has an estimated two million foreign workers who form more than a quarter of the total population of the country, working in the oil industry or as unskilled labour.

24   This area, to the north of Jubayl, has been described as the Newmarket of Saudi Arabia as it is an important breeding area for *dhaluls* or racing camels. To the newcomer it looks desolate with patches of scrub, but it is nevertheless an area of 'prime grazing'! Later when we moved north we were to see the true desolation of the gravel plain that extends from Saudi Arabia into southern Iraq and Kuwait. The high point of the year in Saudi Arabia is undoubtedly the King's Camel Race held in April or May across the plains of

the Nejd north-east of Riyadh. Thousands of *dhaluls* are entered for the race which is run over a gruelling course of 18 kilometres for valuable prizes.

25   The Arabian camel can drink up to 100 litres of water in ten minutes. It stores fat in its hump from which the driver can judge its energy reserves. Camels provide meat and milk, while cloth woven from their coarse hair is used for shelter and clothing. Their skin provides leather for saddles (*hawayya*), waterskins (*girbas*), and belts. The animal's dung is used for fuel, and its urine is used as hair tonic and as a bath to keep flies away from new-born infants. In the past the women of the Murrah tribe used camel's urine to wash their hair, the men to bathe eyes scratched by driven sand, or to wash wounds clean. The camel still constitutes a unit of account, a means of repayment for death or injury. Its rhythmical pace moving at speed is also said to have influenced the lilting metre of Arabic poetry. Poetry became the most developed aspect of Arabian art because it was literally the most portable branch of art for a nomadic race.

26   The jerboa, or desert rat, is one of the desert's most successful creatures. It can jump faster than a man can run, and the soles of its feet are padded with thick hair to absorb the shock of landing. It is nocturnal and feeds on seeds, insects, and plants. Astonishingly, it does not drink water at all, but takes sufficient moisture from the dry plants it eats. The Arabs were at first offended by the description of the famous insignia of 7th Armoured Brigade as a desert rat until it was explained that the creature depicted was not in fact a rat, which is repugnant to an Arab, but a jerboa, which is not.

27   A mosque usually has a minaret (*manarah*, lighthouse), a tower from which the *muezzin* calls the faithful to prayer. The word mosque comes from *masjid*, a word of pre-Islamic origin meaning 'a place to prostrate oneself'. A characteristic of all mosques is their bare simplicity. The interior is empty, though the floor is often covered by richly decorated carpets. There is a formal *minbar* or pulpit which has steps leading up to it and is often elaborately carved. Around the walls there may well be quotations from the *Qur'an* written in the most intricate calligraphy. The central feature of the whole building is the *mihrab*, an alcove which indicates the *qibla*, the direction of prayer. This is of course Mecca, the site of the *Ka'ba*, the black meteorite stone which marks the place where Muhammad first proclaimed the religion of Islam.

28   The cross-bred mare was a sorry sight, but still showed some of the characteristics of the Arabian pure bred, including the dish-shaped nose, the short back, the high-set tail and the flaring nostrils. Nearly every European breed today, from the Lipizzaner to the Percheron, is related to the Arabian horse, and in the early part of this century eastern and central Arabian horses were in great demand by the Indian Army. In Saudi Arabia the tradition of fine breeding continues to this day, particularly in the Nejd region, en couraged by a keen interest in racing.

29   Many soldiers wore *shamaghs* to keep out the dust. A poor-quality Army-issue *shamagh* arrived very late in the campaign. As many soldiers had already bought their own, numerous colour combinations were to be seen with British forces.

30   Attached to the QRIH, one troop per squadron.

31   Initially, the Irish Hussars were assigned an ANGLICO team comprising 15 US Marines. Their principal task was to call in supporting air attacks and direct artillery and naval gunfire. They were an excellent team, led by Captain Mike 'Lumpy' Castagnero, a most popular and amusing officer. On meeting HRH The Prince of Wales, who visited the Irish Hussars on 22 December, one Marine from the ANGLICO team commented: 'It was just great meeting him. We've had the President [George Bush] here but this was the most important person yet. We all love working with the Brits. They keep their feet on the ground and working with them is real sweet.' Later the Regiment lost its ANGLICO team and its link with the US Marine Expeditionary Force when 7th Armoured Brigade became part of VII (US) Corps. An entry in the QRIH war diary reads as follows: 'It was a sad time for the Regiment. We had enjoyed working with the United States Marine Corps. They are fine soldiers, very proud of their heritage and aware of the need for aggressive soldiering. They had adjusted well to armoured warfare and were later to prove their ability when attacking into Kuwait.'

32   The green and white oil barrels bore the word PETROMIN in English and Arabic. The General Petroleum and Mineral Organization of PETROMIN was set up in 1962. It is the state-owned organization responsible for the development, exploitation, and marketing of oil, mineral, and natural gas resources. It operates the Petroline, a crude oil pipeline, which runs for 1,200 kilometres from the oilfields in Al Hasa or Eastern Province to the Red Sea, linking the cities of Jubayl and Yanbu.

33   The black cloak, or *abaaya*, worn by Saudi women has large sleeves and hangs over the head. Unlike the Iranian *chador* it does not cover the face. This was the first and only occasion I saw the black tents of the Bedouin at close quarters during Operation GRANBY, which is an indication of how scarce the desert Arab has become. The Bedouin have declined to less than ten per cent of the population of Arabia, as two per cent of their number a year take up a settled existence in the towns. Oil wealth, the intrusion of the foreigner, modern education and mechanization have all contributed to the decline of the very complex and delicately balanced Bedouin way of life. However, they retain an unequalled reputation as trackers. They can trace a lost man, vehicle or animal with incredible speed, and in fact a Bedouin's word as to a man's weight and size deduced from footprints in the sand is taken as evidence in Saudi courts.

[34] Challenger is a main battle tank, in service with the British Army since 1983. It is equipped with a 120mm rifled gun and carries a crew of four.

[35] 1 (US) Marine Division and 7th Armoured Brigade constructed a large range area near Ras Az Zawr. The British called it Dragoon Range, the Americans Devil Dog Range. Finally it became known as Devil Dog Dragoon Range or D3.

[36] The main threat of 'creepy crawlies' in the Gulf was posed by camel spiders, scorpions and snakes. Camel spiders, known colloquially as 'sun spiders', belong to the *Solifugae* family. The largest species, *Galeodes arabs*, is 5 inches long. The main problem was scorpions of the *Buthidae* family which were known to have stung many Iraqi refugees in one Jordanian camp. By general standards the Gulf scorpions were small, being half the size of the jungle varieties, and without the potency of their sting. There were three varieties of poisonous snake, all of which were dangerous: the carpet viper or saw-scale, *Echis carinatus*, which causes more deaths than any other snake; the nocturnal horned viper, *Cerastes cerastes*, which can grow to over 30 inches; and the rare black desert cobra, *Walterinnesia*, with venom which attacks the muscle and nervous system.

[37] The three regiments of 7th Armoured Brigade were deployed for tactical purposes in 'battle groups' containing different proportions of tanks and mechanized infantry. QRIH Battle Group consisted of three squadrons of tanks but no infantry; Scots DG Battle Group contained three tank squadrons plus one company of 1 Staffords; Staffords Battle Group comprised two infantry companies, plus two tank squadrons (one each from QRIH and Scots DG).

[38] Later identified as a Painted Lady, *Vanessa cardui*, a strong-flying migratory species that arrives in Britain from southern Europe and Africa in June. It is the most widely distributed butterfly in the world.

[39] The word 'Houbara' comes from the houbara bustard, which falconers have reduced almost to extinction in Arabia. Desert Arabs cook bustard by burying them still in their feathers in the hot ashes of a fire.

[40] All the Regiment's tanks were named after Irish towns and villages, the first letter of the name indicating the squadron to which the vehicle belonged.

[41] The flowers included *Nerium oleander*, an evergreen shrub native to the Mediterranean, which is believed to be the 'rose growing by the brooks' of Ecclesiasticus. The butterflies were a Painted Lady and the more vibrantly coloured *Danaeus chrysippus*, an African and Asian relative of the Monarch butterfly of America.

42 The Tapline Road, 'Route Dodge', ran westwards from Dhahran and Al Jubayl along the northern border of Saudi Arabia. The traffic on it was almost nose to tail, and in the words of one staff officer it was 'not a healthy place to be'. Another described it as '...a hair-raising trip which was mostly single lane but had been used by the logistic services of four US Divisions, the Egyptians, the Syrians and the odd Frenchman'. It was littered with vehicles that had broken down or been involved in accidents.

43 An important strand of the Allied deception plan was the decision not to make public the transfer of 1st (BR) Armoured Division from the US Marines to VII (US) Corps on 26 January. During Operation DESERT STORM the US Marines remained on the coast while 1st (BR) Division moved west with VII (US) Corps.

CHAPTER THREE
War

Thursday 17 January 1991 An auspicious day. Op [Operation] DESERT SHIELD became known as Op DESERT STORM. Order to go in signed by [President] Bush on previous Tuesday. An entry in the QRIH diary reads as follows;

> 'At 0430 hours on 17 January the Regiment was awoken. The NBC threat level had changed to high and the Regiment was put on red alert against Iraqi air attacks. At 0120 hours, Iraqi time, Allied Special Forces had carried out attacks against Iraqi anti-aircraft weapons. At 0135 hours 100 Tomahawk cruise missiles were launched at Baghdad attacking C3 [command, control and communication] installations. At 0200 hours Allied aircraft attacked C3 targets, chemical weapon sites and airfields. The war to liberate Kuwait had begun.

You will now be aware what has happened in the Gulf. Our day, on the day that Operation DESERT SHIELD became known as Operation DESERT STORM, began at 0430. We were soon dressed in full NBC kit before dawn. The main fear was a backlash from the Scud sites that may not have been put out of action by air attack. There is no euphoria here. There is no gloating, no sense of self-satisfaction at the destruction of a nation. I hope, for the sake of its members, that the huge Iraqi army capitulates and saves itself rather than resigns itself to a terrible fate. Meanwhile we must press home this attack with the utmost ferocity.

There has been a great deal of tension and uncertainty of what lies ahead, and of chemical weapons in particular. This threat, of course, is now very much reduced, but we have not in any way dropped our guard. Furthermore, we do not yet know if the Iraqi army will crack under the pressure of air power, or will continue to resist totally or in part. Our main concern is the [Iraqi] tank force which is being attacked even at this moment. By the time this letter arrives we will know a good deal more. So, the questions that remain for the moment are these; will we go into action? Will we face chemical attack? Will we face biological attack? Will we advance to take certain areas? Will we advance at all? Or will we simply mop up or have the task of unravelling the grisly aftermath? All I can say is thank God we have the technological edge. If we did not I am not sure I would be writing this letter now! We will just take each day as it comes and one day it will be finished. I gather that the desk merchants at PB17 [Ministry of Defence] are telling me to be back by February 14. But I have absolutely no intention of coming back until this show is over. They live in a bureaucratic haze in a totally different world. Sad news - an RAF Tornado is missing.

Friday 18 January Began taking NAPS [nerve agent pills] from 0600. Eight Scuds against Israel. Targets included Haifa, Nazareth, and Tel Aviv. Total of 17 Scuds launched against Israel and Saudi Arabia. Israeli aircraft reported to be on alert. Seven enemy aircraft shot down. Iraqi 12, 17, 25, and Tawakkulna Divisions hit by air strikes yesterday.[1] 25 Infantry Division and 12 Armoured Division hit by 44 A-10s today.

Saturday 19 January Scuds targeted as follows; three Tel Aviv, one Haifa, one Nazareth, three Dhahran [Saudi Arabia]. In addition three failed in Iraq. Israeli aircraft reported to be on alert but did not respond. Three thousand Allied sorties so far. Seven aircraft lost (four US, two British, one Kuwaiti). Two pilots captured by Iraqis.

Now into day three of the war. It seems like three months! We have been in and out of NBC kit like Yo-Yos. I spoke in a recent letter about the US air response. You will have seen and heard probably more than enough already. It will be going on and on. Meanwhile we are sitting tight. I am now in the HQ. It is 5.45 in the morning. All night since this show began we hear the noise of our own aeroplanes, very high up, moving in to bomb Iraq or Kuwait - or returning.[2] We like that noise! It's certainly my favourite!

It is difficult to get news, but we hear the World Service sometimes which is excellent. It is very detailed and reliable. The measured tones and the famous signature tune at the start, followed by the pips, are something I shall always remember. We also listen to the American forces radio which is excellent. We have basketball on at the moment.

The crew are marvellous. Real Rolls-Royces, all of them. I will know them well by the end of this show. Comradeship and teamwork are the keys. I have never seen it work as well as this before. The mail is being held up both ways because of the volume of operational freight. Got lots of letters the other day. Ten in one go!... It is very warm tonight and I am exhausted. It is very difficult to keep clean. We must be pretty filthy. We wash in cold water from a bucket and do the best we can.[3] The 'luxuries' have gone. Camp 4 has closed down.

In my last letter the war had just begun. I felt sorrow for the Iraqi nation. Since then we have been in and out of NBC kit many times. I must not say anything about intentions, but rest assured the enemy will get a lot more air first. The bombing is continuous. This operation may take much longer than we expect.

All is well. You can be certain that I am in an excellent team. We could not be better led. I have the greatest faith in our leadership and I am sure we will not be committed until everything possible has been done to break the opposition we face in our sector. I'm afraid we must be utterly ruthless now: it's really us or them. I hope that the Iraqis suddenly break but it may take time. I think they will *break and once their back is broken their army will fold. But for the moment, maybe the next month or so, they are very dangerous.*

Sunday 20 January Reveille 0400. Moved to the vehicle RV [Rendezvous] in preparation for the transporter move north to Concentration Area KEYES,[4] south of the Kuwait border. Once at the vehicle pick-up point the Regiment formed up in box formation, by squadrons, in long snaking lines, on ground now deeply gouged and rutted by tank tracks. It was a grey overcast day with flat light. Drivers remained at the RV for the transporter move. The remainder moved by open truck to Jubayl airport where we dived into full NBC kit yet again. The journey took one-and-a-half hours. I was very cold at first, but boiling hot in Jubayl once the sun came up (94 degrees Fahrenheit). We baked on the airport tarmac most of the day, surrounded by forests of helicopters. Jets roared in and out. Thousands of soldiers, registering as mere specks in the distance, boarded aeroplanes heading north. Scores of Hercules and Galaxies [transport aircraft] came and went.

'Road to War'. Tank crews of the Royal Scots Dragoon Guards loading a Challenger onto a transporter, 31 December 1990

Well into the afternoon we were called forward. We were packed into a Hercules like sardines. The ramp closed. Every square inch of space was taken up: the floor too was jammed with men and kit. Men were banked on the ramp itself, crammed together with knees drawn up. We took off and flew in steady level flight. It was very hot. Drenched in sweat, the men slept fitfully. Managed to do a line drawing of the freight bay, in a tiny notebook. Not very good, but the best I could manage. As we approached our destination, KKMC [King Khalid's Military City],[5] over the deafening noise of the engines came the calm measured tones of the pilot with the words; 'We are now descending into KKMC. The very best of luck when you go forward to do what you have to do'. The journey had taken one-and-a-half hours. We arrived at 1645. We were now 240 kilometres north-west of Jubayl. Once there, soldiers stood around in groups. Some laid out sleeping bags on the airport tarmac and rested, with webbing for pillows. Others brewed up, ate compo straight out of tins, or spooned out the contents of MREs (American 'Meals Ready to Eat' or, in the words used by the Americans, 'Meals Rejected by Ethiopians') from small brown plastic containers. Day gave way to dusk, and dusk to night. It became cold. We waited. Most rested uneasily.

Some time during the night came the order to move. Darkened figures, laden with kit, clambered aboard battered buses. We cursed the obstinacy of our unwilling civilian drivers but, suitably cajoled or in some cases goaded, they eventually got on with it and our buses jolted forward. Hours passed. We fell into an exhausted sleep, waking now and then with a start, wondering where we were or when we would arrive. The journey by bus and truck from KKMC was a mix of farce and nightmare. Certainly it was one of the most exhausting trips I have ever made. To our utter astonishment our own bus driver disappeared at one point, ostensibly just for three minutes to obtain authorization to fill a civilian bus with military fuel. He was found one-and-a-half hours later, slumped in a chair in the military barracks nearby. The only reason we found him at all was that there was a full Scud alert which had woken him up. Apparently he had disappeared for a meal and a sleep without telling anyone, least of all us. It is interesting to record that this is how one small part of the 1st British Division was forced to move to a Concentration Area in time of war!

Monday 21 January We expected to reach the vehicle RV at 0200. The bus trip seemed to take forever, and we eventually arrived at 0430. We then marched in column in pitch darkness, like blind men, carrying our kit, in single file. Each element of the Regiment identified its own vehicles but with difficulty. Challenger tanks roared off into the pre-dawn blackness. We eventually arrived at 0630 at the Concentration Area. CETs [combat engineer tractors] dug scrapes and made berms for RHQ tanks and other command troop vehicles. Sheets of anti-NBC material were drawn over the vehicles, which were then camouflaged. We all had splitting headaches, probably from a combination of the effect of the journey and the nerve agent pills we have to take every eight hours. General 'Stormin' Norman Schwarzkopf [the US Operational Commander] announced that Iraq's nuclear and chemical capability has been destroyed.[6] Concentration Area very flat - perfectly level - can see for miles. Stony. Vaguely reminiscent of the farmland of East Anglia: cold and wet. All of us extremely tired.

It's a pretty strange situation. I think my overriding feeling now is that I shall be so glad when it is over. It is pretty tiring. Even if we are not committed at all I shall come back having really pulled out all the stops. When will it end? What will happen? Will I have contributed to my satisfaction in retrospect? I often think of the 'ordinary' things we take too much for granted. Everything after this will be plain sailing.

These are rather momentous days. We made a move recently, part of it by Hercules. The journey was the worst I have ever made. Arrived here absolutely exhausted. Basically, we now sit and wait. Not sure when we move. It is arduous just living, never mind anything else. It is cold and wet. The country here is as flat as a pancake and covered in stones. In a curious way, it reminds me of Norfolk. It is a relief from the sand and the camel-thorn. Actually it is a pretty God-forsaken place. The Oman, by contrast, had some truly spectacular country. So too the Lebanon and Iraq.[7] You will have heard exactly what is going on. We hear the planes going over and continue with plans, moves and so on. Despite the media reports, you need not worry. We know what we are doing and I could not be with a finer 'family'.

Tuesday 22 January Iraqis shot down one of their own helicopters over Kuwait. Five hundred deserters from 18 Infantry Division area. Two thousand, one hundred and thirty Allied air sorties. Main emphasis on Scuds. BDA [Battle Damage Assessment] delayed because of weather. At 2219hrs one Scud was fired at Al Jubayl, but fell into the sea. SAMs and air defence artillery have been firing indiscriminately, indicating that air defence radars, and command and control arrangements are being put out of action. Most enemy airfields still operable. Sea water is being pumped into the Kuwait area, an old Iraqi tactic to impede movement. The movement of oil barges is being reported, possibly to spill oil and then fire it to prevent seaborne landing. Two Scuds against Riyadh and Dhahran. The air campaign has been redirected and switched temporarily to knock out Scud sites as top priority. The technique is to keep aeroplanes airborne while the position of launchers is plotted by AWACS [Airborne Warning and Control System], and then to strike using F-15s followed by B-52s. The priority of targets will be to destroy logistic support and to disrupt the Iraqi main supply route, the Basra-Baghdad road. The real effort against ground forces has not yet started. A-10s are hitting tanks from high altitude using Maverick missiles. Commanding Officer's points: importance of commanders keeping soldiers warm, rested, and interested. The importance of discipline: always keep under camouflage nets. If forced to move in the open, always wear helmets, carry NBC kit and weapon.

Wednesday 23 January Attacks on Republican Guard Force continue. The A-10s have been very successful. Two Scuds fired last night at Tel Aviv, causing 70 casualties. Twenty Iraqi aircraft destroyed in dog fights. Most are still in hardened shelters at air bases. Allies now have air superiority. Iraqi chemical capability has been reduced, but mustard and nerve gas are still being produced. An RPG7 [rocket-propelled anti-tank grenade launcher] washed up on the shore at Jubayl. The Saudis have shot an Iraqi frogman. Baghdad severely hit. No telephones, power, sewage: water is sometimes contaminated. Report that civilians may be drinking untreated water from the Tigris.

[Letter to Mrs A E M Watt] *As for living here, I am recovering a bit from the journey to this place, which is stony and very flat. It is possible to see for miles and miles. We have left the rolling sands behind. The sand is packed down hard, which is bad to sleep on but good for vehicles. As I write, the incessant drone of Allied aeroplanes, high up, moving into Iraq and Kuwait. We don't know what the battle damage is yet because of cloud cover, but I hope we are starting to break the Iraqi army. We don't know how long we will be here, but rest assured we will have more than enough firepower, from air and ground, to cut a swathe through the opposition. The last shreds of comfort, if one could call it that, will be severed when we move, and from then on life will be hard going. I must go to bed soon. We are up very early as you know. I have been very cold at times. The Quartermaster is getting some waterproofs, the lack of which is my main worry. I have been soaked a number of times, which devastates morale. Waterproof clothing is like gold, or unobtainable. I look forward to my Gore-tex arriving more than anything else. It's dry at the moment, but I don't trust the weather, which can be diabolical, or anything else!*

Thursday 24 January Six Scud sites destroyed. Targets were Dhahran (shot down by Patriot) and Riyadh (fell short). Interviewed while sketching, by Martin Bell of the BBC. Also interviewed by *The Daily Mirror* and *The Times*.

We hear the planes going over all the time. At night, and certainly tonight, we hear the bombs detonating. We are well aware of the intelligence and ops picture but we only see our own small corner of this gigantic jig-saw puzzle. It does not always seem real. We listen to the BBC World Service so I have some idea what you are hearing on your news programmes... The gunner crew with whom I live are excellent men, very courteous and helpful. People really come forward in the most amazing way. Nobody holds back.

Friday 25 January It has gone cold and wet again. At one point we had hail. When it rains it really is a God-forsaken place. The Allies captured a small island, which is the first Kuwaiti territory to be re-taken.[8] It appears that the enemy are not moving. BDA is not known because of cloud cover which impedes satellite information. However, Allies are not prepared to fly recce sorties, and thus put aircraft at risk needlessly, when there is the more sensible option of waiting until the weather improves.

A tank commanders' gathering at which various topics were aired, preceded by an excellent summary of the activities of the Press by the BBC reporter, Martin Bell, who once served in the Army, reaching the rank of staff sergeant. He is determined not to be, in his own words, a 'burden', and those in his team will 'dig their own holes' [trenches]. A very able but modest man, who was in fact facing his ninth war. [Martin Bell OBE remained unscathed during the Gulf War, but was later wounded by shrapnel in Sarajevo, Bosnia, in August 1992.]

Saturday 26 January Bright, dry day. Re-packed all my kit and backloaded [sent back to base] all my drawings and excess equipment. Now travelling as light as possible. Have retained sketch-books, pencils and coloured pencils, and camera, plus weapon, helmet, webbing, respirator, bergen [rucksack], and one small camouflage bag. Main worries: no flak jacket, no morphine, and no waterproof kit yet. If I don't get waterproofs for this operation I shall be in serious trouble.

Twenty Iraqi aeroplanes have defected to Teheran. Several aircraft were hit. One crash-landed and burst into flames. Five or six Scuds launched at Israel and Riyadh. Americans sank an oil tanker because it was being used as an observation post. The Iraqis have begun to release thousands of tons of oil into the Persian Gulf from an oil terminal, blaming the Americans and causing an ecological disaster. There is no end to [Saddam] Hussein's madness.[9]

You can rest assured that this operation has been planned in meticulous detail. I am quite certain we will knock these clowns for six. 8.20 at night in the back of an APC. It's getting cold. It actually hailed today. Can you believe it? This is a God-forsaken place in the rain. Most of the soldiers want to get in and get out.

I am not ready yet! I am still battling with my kit. The dilemma of what to take and what to leave. Equipment - impedimenta, becomes a nightmare. The less there is the better but I have my art kit and I don't want to leave it behind. This is the last place where I can backload any of my kit onto a truck. I will see it later but it will be after the push. On the art side I shall take camera; sketch-books, one big, one small; graphite pencils, and a box of coloured crayons.

I cannot say where we are or when we go. Perhaps some at home may have some curious notion that this is a great picnic in which we strain at the leash to take part in some glorious crusade. Nothing could be further from the truth. We are ready to go - yes - but everyone is very level-headed, very steady, very conscious of the test ahead, and focussing on the problem in the minutest detail.

The safe, easy life seems to be part of a different planet! Things will take on a new meaning from now on. Apparently ordinary things like a walk to the post box, attending the school play or a pantomime at Christmas; and a million and one other things.

[Letter to Mrs A E M Watt] *Am doing a radio watch at the moment. It is nearly 9 in the evening. Most people are in bed by 7.30 because it's black at 6.15. We are up at 5.30 in the morning. These are pretty intense days. We can really see comradeship working here. One sees leaders leading and soldiers being professional to the 'n'th degree - unprompted, because we've got to get it right. The smallest details are checked and re-checked. And training continues, and tactical procedures and drills are repeated again and again. I can see now why we train this way. I can also see that the training I have done all my professional life has always been on exactly the right lines. It is extraordinary the things that are important now - the role of the Padre, the importance of mail, the need to keep warm and dry, the value of morale, the importance of personal organization - knowing exactly where everything is in the dark, and a host of other things.*

Sunday 27 January It pelted with rain all night. We squelch around in mud. The scene is one of misery but morale is high. The order of the day is to keep warm and dry. Soldiers check respirators, clean weapons, and unload magazines to take the strain off the springs. It is damp and cold. There is enough light inside vehicles to check weapons and equipment. Rain continues and occasionally a deluge of water is heard, as water that has gathered in small ponds on the canvas roofs of our shelters is removed. Attended 'prayers' [the daily 'Orders Group'] at 1230 followed by a church service. Very cold wet day. Spent the morning writing some notes on how to apply deception and psyops [psychological operations] to future operations. Then became pretty tired. Some of my photographs arrived.

Those ghastly photographs of downed pilots today. This man [Saddam Hussein] *will pay a terrible price. That sort of thing makes us even more determined to break their army and finish this war. Most think it will take months rather than days. I hope it will be somewhere in between. Whatever the armchair tacticians are saying at home and whatever happens, you can tell them that the atmosphere here is sombre but not subdued. These are professional men going about their business calmly and efficiently.*

Comradeship and teamwork count for everything, cutting right across rank and class. There will be no gloating in victory, just a sadness at the cost. There is no doubt that, man for man, our Army and our Armed Services have no equal. I thought I ought to record these thoughts because when I am asked what I felt at the time someone can read these notes. Many servicemen must have experienced exactly the same feelings through the centuries, but each would express them a different way. Meanwhile we wait. The clutter of life has been cut away.

Arthur Denaro is a free-thinking, imaginative and very high-calibre leader. He is absolutely terrific and the morale of his men is tremendous. The one thing that stands out above everything is the fact that he cares. He cares for every man and he knows them all inside out. At 'stand to' at dawn and dusk, even in the vilest of vile weather, he will visit every man in every trench. He always has a friendly word. 'How's it going boys?' is his usual greeting. That's how to lead.

Monday 28 January Seven Floggers [Russian-built Iraqi aircraft] shot down. It is believed that Iraq may resort to the use of chemical and biological weapons. Good weather: cold but clear. Drew the crew of Commanding Officer's tank, *Churchill*. The name refers to Winston Churchill, who was Colonel of the Regiment from 1958 to his death in 1965, and also to a small village in Co. Donegal. Very tired today. Started taking nerve agent pills every eight hours, following reports that Saddam Hussein had loaded aircraft with chemical weapons. A number of Iraqi aircraft have defected to Teheran. These aircraft will probably be impounded by Iran until the end of the war, as the Iranians have made a pledge to the UN to do so. Also the aircraft lack spares and some are damaged. American planes have destroyed the oil pumping station to staunch the deluge of oil into the Persian Gulf. The overall intelligence picture is somewhat confused.

Tuesday 29 January Went to Headquarters 1st (BR) Division. Later [at the Headquarters of the Irish Hussars] sketched an improvised shower in the form of a fire bucket with a shower attachment underneath.

Very quick note. Very late at night. Difficult to know what to say. We are getting on with life. At last it looks as though we have air supremacy, but a wounded animal is always dangerous. We continue to make preparations. After all the uncertainties we have been through, it is strange to think that soon we go. I hope that as many Iraqis as possible are spared. It is not their fault: it is the fault of one maniac. I heard some Beethoven today. It seemed extraordinarily peaceful... Mail is by far the greatest thrill here.

At Divisional Headquarters today. I am sitting in a chair for once, at a six-foot wooden table. Am not used to tables or chairs any more! It is still very cold at night, but I have my two waistcoats and two Norwegian jerseys which are excellent. We are still getting a certain amount of rain. When it rains here it is really foul. Mud knee deep, rather like scenes from the First World War, but not so extensive, just in the area we live in. We live in holes surrounded by mounds of earth - berms or bunds. The weather will start getting warm again in about a month's time. One wonders what will happen in that time? I have to go and have my second BW jab now: I'm like a pin cushion. The things I have learnt here...! I even know how to set up an IV drip!

Wednesday 30 January Practised minefield breach by day and by night, for the impending offensive. Fighting at Al Khafji to the east where a US Marine border post was forced to withdraw. Sitrep [situation report] on Al Khafji incident as at 2000hrs last night; Saudi Arabian National Guard unit and US reconnaissance unit taken on by an Iraqi mechanized battalion. It is now possible that more than one brigade may be involved. Iraqi National Grid destroyed. Iraq's electricity now operating at ten per cent, using generators. Two bridges over the Euphrates destroyed. In the next 24 hours there will be 2,854 air sorties. Thirty-two B-52s will attack Hammurabi Division [Republican Guard] tanks.[10] A million pounds of explosive will be dropped. Blue Air [Allied air power] is now switching to the battle preparation phase, the initial aim of which is to reduce enemy artillery by 90 per cent. At sea six Iraqi ships destroyed, five of them by British Lynx [helicopters] using Sea Skua [anti-ship missiles]. Ref the Khafji battle, US have taken 76 POW [prisoners of war], Saudis have taken 36. US dead ten, with four wounded.[11]

The Iraqis made some probing attacks along the border this morning. We put in a lot of aircraft against them and destroyed most of their armour. The B-52s have gone in today to break up the tank reserves. One million pounds weight of bombs and 2,000 aircraft sorties today alone. We hear aircraft going over constantly. Just heard that the US Marine Corps are engaging the Iraqis somewhere. Our pilots report oil refineries in Iraq on fire and two bridges over the Euphrates have gone.

Thursday 31 January *I managed to draw Arthur Denaro's tank today. It's called* Churchill. *We all have colds and are feeling a bit 'fluey' - the direct result not of flu, but of our second BW jab and these bloody nerve agent pills. We take the latter every eight hours. We all have to remind each other: have you taken your NAPS? We are woken in the dead of night to take the wretched things. Am sitting in the back of the gunner APC. It's 9 in the evening. Wearing my two Norwegians, a shamagh and* *desert combats... To better things. I heard some Mozart the other day: a horn concerto. Creativity seems our only hope amidst this hideous destruction. One searches for tranquillity...[12] I want this to be over. We all do. We want to get the hell out of this place! But morale is very good. You can tell anyone in England there is no glamour in this. It is basic hard living: very strenuous. It's hard on the nerves. All we want is to finish. But all is well, this is a marvellous team.*

Friday 1 February Thirty thousand Allied air sorties so far. More than 40 aircraft destroyed. F-117 Stealth aircraft have destroyed over 50 hardened bunkers sheltering aircraft. A number of aircraft have defected to Iran. Thirty-six road and rail bridges destroyed. Large casualties inflicted on tailbacks on MSRs [main supply routes]. Approximately 50 Scud and over 100 ammo sites destroyed. Three hundred sorties against convoys, FROG [Russian-built Iraqi missiles] and armour. Republican Guard have been hit by 455, 350, and 470 tons of explosives on consecutive days. In period 28-30 January, over 100 tanks and artillery pieces destroyed. Sketched four Irish Hussar officers seated beside the Commanding Officer's tank, *Churchill*. The officers were Colonel Arthur Denaro, Major Mark O'Reilly, Captain Andrew Cuthbert, and Captain Robert Hutton. Had a filthy cold and felt really quite ill. It may be the result of the second BW jab, and the nerve agent pills every eight hours.

I seem to be hungry permanently. I eat biscuits, chocolate, mixed fruit pudding, oatmeal blocks, anything I can lay my hands on. Whenever I have a meal, I cram myself, rather like a working Labrador after a long day in the field! We have steaming mugs of hot tea at the moment and breakfast is on. The best meal of the day.

Food was second only to mail in importance. The best meal of the day was undoubtedly breakfast, coming as it did immediately after the morning 'stand to' when most of us felt decidedly jagged, and the older one was, the more jagged one felt! But breakfast put us 'right'! It was a lorry driver's dream - and a doctor's nightmare. Plates and mess-tins would arrive groaning with eggs, fried bread, baked beans, sausages, and compo 'bacon grill', sizzling in a sea of oil. We wolfed down these 'cholesterol specials' without fear for the future or absurd worries about waistlines! It was interesting how most of us developed a liking for strong tastes and spicy food, apparently a well-known physiological fact associated with desert life. Fruit became rare and precious. On one occasion I found a Jaffa orange in the back of an APC. I am ashamed to say I ate it immediately! Shortly afterwards I was made aware, in polite but restrained tones, that this orange belonged to someone else. The unfortunate owner, Sergeant Lakeland 40 Field Regiment RA [Royal Regiment of Artillery], quite rightly took a pretty dim view of this act of piracy, particularly as both he and his excellent crew had looked after me magnificently for months on end! My sense of guilt finally drove me to launch a lightning night raid on Zero Hotel [the Officers' Mess tent], in order to liberate an orange to replace this severe loss! Food parcels from home represented the two principal pleasures of desert life, food and mail, rolled into one. Biscuits and chocolate in particular were singled out as the principal quarry and hunted down.

Have now been here two months. It feels as though the war has been going for about two years. I have got a filthy cold and don't feel very well, but it's a privilege to be with these soldiers. You can rest assured that this bloody little fiend is not going to snarl up our lives!

Saturday 2 February Feeling better. Enemy in the Wadi Al Batin number about 1,000 tanks, which have been broken up by air power. BDA: large explosion seen during air raid on Tawakkulna Division believed to be a major ammo dump exploding. Bombing continues on 10, 12, 17, and Tawakkulna Divisions, the aim being to reduce all Divisions to 50-60 per cent CE [combat effectiveness]. NBC threat remains high and chemical attack must be expected. Bombing of 17 Division continues.

Attended a regimental church service taken by Father Sean Scanlon and the Brigade Anglican Padre, Alan Price. Drew a very small sketch of Father Sean. Captain Tom Beckett spoke on the latest intelligence picture.

An interrogation team from the Brigade Headquarters discussed the handling of POWs and Colonel Denaro gave his final address to the regiment. In the afternoon I made one or two sketches of camouflaged vehicles in Battle Group Headquarters. The wind was blowing hard and the visibility was poor. B-52 raids continued all night.

Have just washed some clothes. Long gone are the days of showers. We wash as best we can but we are probably pretty dirty! No doubt an outsider can pick us up a mile away! It's all very basic stuff. We live under our cam nets in the back of vehicles, on the ground outside, or in trenches. It is a joy to get away from everyone to think in silence just occasionally. I truly know the meaning of peace now. Those who thirst for war are round the bend. I often think of gentle, civilized things: fishing, the countryside, houses, music, paintings; but in the distance is the ever-present sound of bombs exploding with a rumbling thud. But for now we wait.

Never mention the word 'gas' to me again! When I speak to the younger soldiers, it comes out in conversation that they do worry about coming out of this thing in one piece. Since I am so much older,[13] I try to make light of it and tell them that all will be well, but of course no one can be sure. The Iraqis do not seem to be folding yet. We are cutting off their logistic, command and control, and communication systems first; then hitting their strategic and tactical reserves and then their ground forces along the border. No secret there. I would like to see mass defections, mass surrenders, to indicate that the Iraqi army is about to crack, but I don't think we will see that for a while and it will not be a pushover. We all expect a long, hard fight.

Sunday 3 February *Had a Regimental Service today with the whole Regiment there. These are very moving occasions. Seeing all those faces, mostly very young ones, about to go into battle. It's always been like that I suppose, but each generation has to face it - only once in most cases, thank God. I must go now, it's pretty late. I will tell you when we go, but by then we will have gone. It will be the beginning of the end for Iraq.*

'GAS! GAS! GAS!' A soldier of 7th Armoured Brigade
during an NBC alert, January 1991

Monday 4 February Received detailed assessments of total Iraqi equipment destroyed in KTO in terms of main battle tanks, armoured personnel carriers, and artillery pieces. In 6 Armoured Division, one brigade headquarters received a direct hit. One B-52 reported to have crashed in the Indian Ocean returning from a raid. Five men missing initially, but three crew rescued later. The plane went down 30 minutes from Diego Garcia.[14] A Cobra [American helicopter] crashed, killing two.

Day 19 of the war. During the night the huge American battleship USS *Wisconsin* moved closer inshore to Kuwait City and began pounding prefabricated hardened bunkers with one-and-a-half ton shells from her 16-inch guns. An American shuttle bus was ambushed by terrorists in the [Saudi] port of Jeddah. Air sorties flown today against the RGFC [Republican Guard Force Command] areas as follows: Nebuchadnezzar Division, 12 B-52s using 540 bombs; Medina Division, 180 F-16s, six A-6s;[15] Hammurabi Division, six B-52s, 72 F-16s, four Tornados; Tawakkulna Division three B-52s. All main bridges are destroyed and sorties continuing on pontoon bridges. One of the missing crewmen from the downed B-52 was found dead today. Iraqi desalination plants may be at 50 per cent capacity, oil production is low. Saw three B-52s flying over our position, leaving behind white vapour trails.

Tuesday 5 February Allied air campaign stepped up against RGFC and regular armoured units. Air sorties are going in at the rate of one per minute. US Naval Harriers [aircraft] have destroyed 25 tanks. Saudis are attempting to prevent the oil slick from entering the large water desalination plant near Al Jubayl.

1st (BR) Division conducted Exercise DIBDIBAH DRIVE, a complicated exercise to practise the move of the Division through a minefield breach, in preparation for Operation DESERT STORM. Moved to start point and, once there, slept beside the vehicles which were formed up in long columns. Sketched Lieutenant Alex Cormack's tank, *Drogheda*. The tank was fully up-armoured [given additional armour protection], with extra fuel drums attached. Began move to Staging Area at 0841. Transferred from APC to *Beechill*, a Bedford fuel vehicle, at the invitation of Captain Arthur Currie, Commander A1 Echelon [vehicles and stores used to re-supply fighting troops]. Observed this extraordinary move from the inside of the cab. The driver, Trooper Howe, had driven non-stop all the previous day and worked without pause throughout the night, re-fuelling tanks while their crews slept. He was the epitome of the British fighting soldier - tough, resilient, infinitely patient, and best when the chips are down.

During this exercise I had a nasty shock. At 3 o'clock in the morning came the order to move. I was at the head of the column of vehicles, separated from *Beechill*. Already the trucks were on the move, large dark rectangular shapes lurching across the desert in long lines, showing minimal light, with despatch riders on motor cycles threading their way in and out of the column. I had just enough time to find *Beechill* as it moved past and scramble into the cab, festooned with equipment. A few minutes later I checked my equipment. My respirator was missing! I had lost my most precious possession. I must have dropped this bar of gold as I climbed into the cab. Now it lay somewhere out in the desert. There was no going back, and I cursed my stupidity!

The column rolled along inexorably on its designated route, through check-point after check-point, following a plan worked out in meticulous detail over many months by the divisional staff. Hundreds of vehicles snaking across the desert. Occasionally a helicopter accompanied us for a moment and then banked out of sight. Vehicles were not spread out at the normal convoy distance but bunched together. It was very strange to go against all the rules of training, but there was no need in view of total Allied air supremacy - and thank God for it. We were not far from the Iraqi border. The desert here was covered in black and white stones, with virtually no plants of any kind.

Wednesday 6 February Allied bombers continue to bomb the RGFC and Marines continue to practice amphibious landings. Fifty thousand air sorties by Allies to date. A Royal Engineer tank was blown to pieces in an accident.[16] The largest piece left was the size of a chair. One man suffered burst ear drums; five others were wounded by shrapnel. The rehearsal finished at 0830 after a very tiring night move through a Staging Area, a simulated minefield breach, organized by the Americans, to an FUP [Forming Up Place]. There the exercise ended.

Thursday 7 February Reinforcement of Tri-Border Area continues with a general movement of Iraqi forces to the south-west. This means the defensive line is being extended into Iraq. It also means that gaps are being created as the Iraqi army becomes overstretched. The

Khafji action produced 400 POWs, including four colonels, one brigadier, and many other officers of field rank. Fifty-one APCs were destroyed and 19 captured. Iraqis suffering from poor food, low morale, and shortage of water.

Made two sketches of two sentries in a trench at dawn. Did a radio watch in Battle Group Headquarters from 1800 to 2100.

It is time we got on with this show and finished the Iraqis off. We have all had enough of them now. This really must be the biggest hole in the world. We did a practice run the other day. It was only overnight but was absolutely exhausting. We have just heard the report of the mortar attack on Downing St.[17] No peace anywhere at the moment. I am in the back of an APC: the engine is running so we can boil up some water for a cup of tea. The light is pretty bad in here. A soldier is reading an out-of-date copy of The Daily Mirror.

Friday 8 February Two 15,000 pound bombs were dropped from a C-130 [Hercules] or Galaxy on the front line defences of the Iraqi 31 and 36 Divisions. No BDA yet. Tawakkulna Division believed to have lost a large number of APCs.

Lance-Bombardier Ayling RA
copying out signal instructions, 7 February 1991

Hammurabi and Medina Divisions a small number of tanks each. Adnan and Nebuchadnezzar Divisions still combat effective.[18]

Iraqi airfields very severely hit. Air defence threat written off. Combat air patrols now stationed permanently over Baghdad. Allied aircraft are able to re-fuel over the city with impunity. Seventy to 80 per cent of oil refineries believed to be destroyed... The battle preparation phase has begun. B-52s deliver attacks every 30 minutes, 24 hours a day, on Republican Guard and other targets. Allies now using 15,000 pound bombs against Iraqi front line defences and, specifically, minefields.[19] Psyops [Psychological Operations] continue.

Saturday 9 February Allied aircraft have severely reduced the tanks of the Tawakkulna Division. Spent the day sketching at A Squadron QRIH. Sketched Corporal Dornan writing a letter on the cupola of the Squadron leader's tank, *Antrim*. The Squadron leader of A Squadron is Major Hugh Pierson. Then sketched Trooper Hermon of 2 Troop, on top of the tank *Autherstown*, writing a letter. Thence to another tank of the same troop, where I sketched Lance-Corporal Coomber cooking stew for the crew.

I know it will be over one day, but we feel as though we have been at war for literally years already. It's only three weeks but it seems infinitely longer. The one big worry is the chemical threat. Whatever happens I can tell you it frightens us and I am not too proud to say that.[20] But chemical is a terror weapon. It is fairly difficult to use effectively and I hope we will be able to say in retrospect that the danger was overrated. I have a curious belief that will be so.

Sunday 10 February Sketched a church service taken by Father Sean Scanlon. Father Sean was wearing a bright green stole, which is the liturgical colour used between Epiphany and Lent. I also sketched the six-foot table which served as an altar, on which there were a prayer

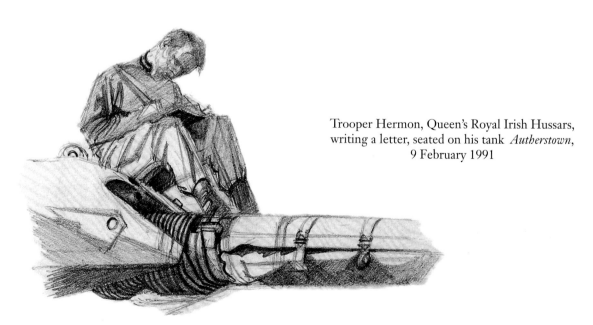

Trooper Hermon, Queen's Royal Irish Hussars,
writing a letter, seated on his tank *Autherstown*,
9 February 1991

book, a crucifix and bottles for wine and water. Thence to A Squadron to sketch an Orders Group, presided over by Major Hugh Pierson. I then sketched the Troop leader of 2 Troop, Captain David Madden, and his troop sergeant, playing chess.

Monday 11 February Study day for tank commanders. I spoke on deception and set up a Challenger decoy tank screen.

Tuesday 12 February Deserters state that morale, even in RGFC, is low, with transistor radios banned, no access to BBC World Service. Two Scuds fired against Israel and one against Riyadh. Observed a smoke generator demonstration by tanks of the Irish Hussars. Some Americans from the Dreadnought Battalion visited the Regiment and rode on D Squadron Challengers. Saw a game of baseball with Staff Sergeant Niven wielding a bat. Went to Scots DG for supper. It was the most relaxed evening I have known here. Strange to enjoy a normal conversation about swimming in Australia and safaris in Kenya.[21] Returned to QRIH leaguer at 2230. I then spent until 0130 writing some notes on deception for Scots DG to present to them the following day.

Wednesday 13 February Steady stream of deserters. Estimated that about 120 Iraqi aircraft have been destroyed in hardened sites. The identification sign for British tanks is to be an inverted V painted on turrets and side armour with red fluorescent panels on turrets. Did a spell as watch-keeper from 1500 to 1800. Met[eorology]: dawn 0611, sunrise 0635.

It is St Valentine's Day tomorrow, so I'm told! The planes roar overhead into Kuwait and Iraq. Still we wait, train, rehearse, prepare. It's been a testing time and hard on the nerves. It is a curious situation. Ourselves waiting here with such carnage and devastation to our north. We will be involved in it at some stage, fighting or observing - who knows. You might wonder exactly where I shall be in this battle. My view is that since I am here I must be up front. It's no good being at the back is it?! I am writing this at night in the back of an APC. I hear the World Service in the background. Watch-keepers are manning the wirelesses. Some sleep, others come and go as watches and sentries change. Plans are made for the next morning well into the night. We are pretty cramped. There is kit every-where but it is very organized: helmets, respirators, flak jackets, weapons all to hand, day and night.

Thursday 14 February Flash-hoods and gloves are to be issued to tank crews. Call signs of Irish Hussar tanks are to be displayed on the two external fuel drums attached to the back of each tank. For example in the case of Call Sign 11B, the figures 11 will be shown on the left hand fuel drum, the letter Bravo on the right hand fuel drum. Seven thousand Day-Glo air recognition panels are being flown out from England. Moved from Concentration Area KEYES towards Assembly Area RAY.[22] Photographed a Regimental Orders Group and three B-52s flying north-west to attack Iraqi positions in the Tri-Border Area.

Very happy St Valentine's Day! I am sitting in the sun just outside the cam-net that covers the vehicles. It's pleasantly warm. I have my helmet on, NBC kit at hand, and weapon across my knees. We are about to make a move. One of a series of moves. You will know from the news when we go. At this stage we still do not know. Security is very tight, thank God. The weather is starting to warm up but is still cold at night. We will be in NBC kit for this operation. Let's hope they don't spray the damn stuff around on our line of advance. Rest assured we are well kitted out. We will have helmets, flak jackets, and flameproof coveralls. Tank crews will have flash hoods and gloves. NBC! - wait - just had to go into full NBC kit because this maniac has launched another missile somewhere. Back, sitting in my NBC kit, writing. The vehicles are de-camouflaged, engines running, ready to move. Meanwhile Scots DG Challengers thunder past in clouds of dust. Scud fired at Jubayl but destroyed by Patriot.

Friday 15 February Exercise DIBDIBAH CHARGE, the rehearsal exercise for Operation DESERT SABRE, continued.[23] Began 2200hrs on 14 February. Moved all night through a Concentration Area and an FUP. Once firm [formed up and in position], 7th Armoured Brigade attacked two objectives - AMBER 1 and AMBER 2. Thence to an Assembly Area [RAY] in preparation for Operation DESERT SABRE. It was a grim night in the back of an APC with three others. Lay on the floor amidst a sea of equipment and ammunition. The dust was choking and it was very noisy. There was no way of knowing exactly where we were, or how long we were to travel. Maps were in short supply. Climbed out at dawn tired and stiff. Drew a sketch of the Command Troop Sultan [armoured command vehicle], with the Colonel's tank 11B in the middle distance, and other tanks in the far distance. Moved to the Assembly Area after hearing the news that Saddam Hussein had called for peace. There was jubilation for a few hours, and a great sense of relief and relaxation. We all suddenly felt safe in the knowledge that we would all rejoin our families. The greatest worry of all, the chemical threat, had vanished. The younger soldiers were particularly relieved; it was they who became the quietest of all as when, later, we reflected on the news that Saddam Hussein's ludicrous 'peace' plan had been rejected by the Allies. As night fell, we began once again to tighten our belts and to dispel any thoughts other than that we would go in as planned. It was a cold night.

Started a long move about 10 last night. Moved all night. I was in the back of an APC filled with dust. It was also very cold. Sitting beside the vehicle now. Time 1.30 in the afternoon. We're all pretty tired. Always seem to be uncomfortable. This is a pretty grisly business and we haven't started the hard bit yet. Exercise, train, rehearse, brief, study, again and again, an endless repetition, but always seeking perfection. These boys will know everything there is to know by the time we go... We had the euphoric news that Iraq had agreed to pull out of Kuwait. I immediately thought thank God we've managed to pull through this thing. Then the realization that nothing has changed. That ground forces will be committed. It hit the younger chaps quite hard. But I still think the Iraqis will fold.

Saturday 16 February By dawn the time for reflection was over. Soldiers had once again locked onto the fact that we would attack the Iraqi army shortly. Humour and resolve returned. Men went about the well-rehearsed routines of cleaning weapons, checking equipment, and preparing themselves for the days ahead. Scud attack on Jubayl which was destroyed by Patriot. General Sir Peter de la Billière promised that the offensive would be 'short and sharp', and that he would '...get the Division home very soon afterwards'. The plan now is that I travel with the B Squadron FOO [Forward Observation Officer], Captain Richard Bryson RHA [Royal Horse Artillery], and his Warrior. I will join the Warrior in the Staging Area. There is a 24-hour delay for the planned gun raid. Operation DESERT SABRE will go ahead as planned. From the American news briefing covering the period 1800hrs 15 February to 1800hrs 16 February: two A-10s lost in 24 hours. Total Allied aircraft shot down so far is 29. One A-10 shot down a helicopter. Thirty-six fixed-wing enemy aircraft and six helicopters also shot down. Two thousand, six hundred air sorties in the last 24 hours. Total of 76,000 air sorties flown to date.[24]

I have been doing as many drawings as I can, concentrating entirely as you suggested on figures and soldiers - the human element. I have drawn soldiers on tanks, writing letters home, crews playing cards or chess, Orders Groups and church services... I must say, I have been frightened a number of times in this show already. I do not worry particularly about hostile artillery fire or mortars, or machine guns, because I know about all that from Oman, but I do worry about gas! I never wish to hear the word 'gas' again!

We have just finished a pretty hard exercise which is actually a rehearsal for our part in this show. General de la Billière has told us it will be short and sharp, and that he will get us back shortly afterwards. That is encouraging. Allied planning has been absolutely meticulous, so please take comfort in that. And when we go, our firepower will be devastating. Our equipment is superb and our logistic system is excellent. Our leadership is unequalled. 1 Armoured Division may be small, but its quality in terms of morale, leadership, and equipment is without peer in this theatre. I think Challenger and the infantry Warrior will prove themselves in battle many times over. And the skill of the crews will be decisive.

Sunday 17 February Last night attacks by Allied forces included seven separate engagements.[25] These involved Allied tanks, artillery, and Apache helicopters. Attended a regimental church service taken by Father Sean Scanlon, the last Sunday before Operation DESERT SABRE, the 1st (BR) Armoured Division offensive to liberate Kuwait. Spent three hours watch-keeping. Drew a watch-keeper's view of the inside of a Sultan Command Vehicle, showing a map of Exercise DIBDIBAH CHARGE, the rehearsal exercise for Operation DESERT SABRE.

Last night it was very windy, with the camouflage net billowing all over the place. It spat with rain at dawn. All night aircraft flew to and from Iraq and Kuwait. We are so used to it now. Now and then the sky would light up as bombs exploded. We wait. It is 8.40 at night: fairly late for us. I ought to go out into the darkness and find my bed. Living is pretty basic. I should think we are all pretty heaving. I certainly haven't had a shower for about two months. More aircraft overhead. They fly quite high.

My ideas are flitting from one line of thought to the next so the result is rather disjointed. This is partly because I am being distracted by this and that, and partly because this vehicle is so damned uncomfortable. My back hurts. This place is flat and cold and desolate. One wonders sometimes why we should be fighting for this dreadful place! ...There are times when I think of our visits to Fortnum's. It could be on a different planet!

Monday 18 February An Apache helicopter roared overhead. Began the day by making a drawing of the Headquarters. Then sketched a captain of 22 Special Air Service Regiment writing some notes at 'Morning Prayers'. Then attended a briefing on Ops and Int[elligence] subjects. Captain Nick Marshallsay, 2 RTR [2nd Royal Tank Regiment], a most gifted natural actor and mimic, gave a light and very amusing presentation on the subject of Iraqi strengths and weaknesses. The latter include low morale, poor communications, and divided leadership.

Americans dropping fuel-air explosive to destroy minefields, and B-52s continue to attack Republican Guard Force. Apache [helicopter] raids up to 150 kilometres over the border. Biological factories destroyed, but chemical attack remains a strong possibility. Colonel Denaro addressed the Regiment explaining the overall Allied plan and the part to be played by VII (US) Corps of which the Irish Hussars were part. He ended his address to the Regiment emphasizing two points: firstly, the importance of discipline, which he had stressed from the moment the Regiment arrived at Al Jubayl four months earlier, and which he continued to stress as the cornerstone which would 'carry the Regiment through'. Secondly, the fact that *every* man in the Battle Group is important and *every* man has an important part to play. His final words were to this effect; 'You are all good, *very* good - God bless you all'.

Tuesday 19 February Collected some stones from Assembly Area RAY. Attended a presentation by Captain Richard Bryson on subject of artillery. Heavy bombing of Baghdad overnight. Apache helicopters launched a raid on 45 Infantry Division. Played 'Monopoly' with the crew of the Warrior. To bed.

The politicians are wavering. Do we go or not? I have always had a feeling that the Iraqis, despite the massive size of their army, will cave in.

Wednesday 20 February At 0400 I saw some very bright flashes of light due north of our leaguer. At first I thought it was an artillery barrage. I then saw very clearly-defined forked lightning accompanied by the heavy rumbling of thunder. At 0430 it began to spit with rain. Shortly afterwards the heavens opened and a wind of Biblical fury raced through the leaguer, splintering camouflage poles and hurling rain-soaked camouflage nets through lean-to sleeping shelters. I had no shelter that night. My camp bed filled with water and all my belongings were soaked through. I managed to disentangle myself from the camouflage net that now lay flat across my camp bed. Bundling a Norwegian jersey and a Barbour waistcoat into the middle of my sleeping bag to keep them dry, I ran barefoot to the Warrior, soaked through and freezing. Dressed only in my underpants, I crammed myself inside the vehicle, and with my feet now in the sleeping bag, pulled on my Norwegian, the waistcoat and my *shamagh*. 'Stand to' came and went. The crew took my sleeping bag and liner away and dried them on the back decks of the Squadron leader's Challenger. A fresh breeze sprang up. Soon all my kit was hanging on the inside of the camouflage net, now re-assembled, drying out.

Attended a briefing by the Brigade Commander, Brigadier Cordingley. The address was pitched at exactly the right level and was very well received, being at once straightforward, honest, amusing, and poignant.[26] The Commander ended his address with a quote from the four final lines of Kipling's famous poem 'If'. About this time one could detect a change of atmosphere. Gone was the need for commanders to chivvy and chase. Now was the time to build men's confidence and settle them. Mild rebukes replaced strong words or withering rockets. Training and rehearsals were complete. The scene was set.

It's pitch black outside. We had a terrible storm last night. We all got absolutely soaked. The sooner we get out of this place the better! The politicians continue to wrangle over whether we fight or not. I will be so pleased when this is over. But don't worry; I am in good hands here.

Thursday 21 February The Regiment held the final training day for tank commanders. The Commanding Officer ended his address with this instruction to his Battle Group: 'keep steady' and 'keep very calm on the air'.

Liaison Officer Major Tim Bidie attending a
briefing, 21 February 1991

Friday 22 February (G-2) [G Day minus 2] Drew a sketch of Irish Hussars doing early morning PT [Physical Training]. Despite talk of peace, Friday 22 February has been declared 'G-2', 'G Day' being the day the Allies are to advance to liberate Kuwait.[27] British guns in action on previous day in cross-border gun raid. Twenty-three guns, 345 rounds at three targets, five rounds per target. Gunner Keegan died. He was run over during a move from one gun position to another. On the night of the appalling storm, two 15,000 pound bombs were dropped on Iraqi 48 Division defences. They must have thought the world had come to an end.[28] 101 Air Battalion attacked bunkers 250 kilometres into enemy territory and took 476 POWs. This was 70 kilometres west of our own position. 1st US Cavalry mounted a recce by force, destroying 50 artillery pieces, five tanks, and taking 11 POWs. One Scud fired at KKMC and two at Bahrain. All shot down by Patriot missiles. Made sketches of Headquarters B Squadron. Subject was the Squadron leader, Major David Swann, marking maps for Operation DESERT SABRE before issuing orders for the operation itself.[29]

Just got up. Time 0550. Am in the back of the Warrior. A lot of Allied bombing this morning. The guns are in action too, but still we wait. Heavy thuds continue in the background. At 8 o'clock our time last night, that hideous dictator was supposed to give his response to the peace proposal. We don't know what was said yet; nor do we know if it is peace or war. The latter we assume. We have been up and down so many times it seems like a lifetime. Ground forces are officially on 'Hold'. But, if certain points are not agreed, we go in. This will all be very old news when it arrives, but it serves to

M109 howitzers of 137 (Java) Battery RA in action on the Iraq-Saudi Arabia border, 21 February 1991

illustrate the up-down nature of emotions at this end. There are those, for professional reasons, who really wish to fight on the basis of all that training and never the test. But there is also the other side of the coin. If we achieve victory without a shot being fired by the ground forces, then we could go home without casualties. One Allied life taken in this place is not worth a thousand Iraqis, because of their duplicity and their total disregard for any form of decent civilized behaviour. Their leaders are the scum of the earth. It is a cold, damp, grey morning. The sun is not yet up, but struggling to emerge over the horizon. If peace comes it will give me more opportunities to draw, because I won't have to jump in and out of my NBC kit every two minutes! No good speculating, I will take life as it comes. Then let's get on with something sensible! Art, travel, racing: I can't wait.

Saturday 23 February (G-1) Four Scuds directed against KKMC, Riyadh, Bahrain, Al Jubayl. Saddam Hussein rejected the peace proposal. Today is G-1. G Day is Sunday 24 February. Noted the Regimental Collect of the QRIH in my sketch-book. It reads: 'Almighty God, whose hands have fashioned us, remember, we pray thee for good The Queen's Royal Irish Hussars and all who serve with us. Keep us mindful of former valour and grant us thy grace that, whatsoever our hands shall find to do for thee, we may do it with all our might, through Jesus Christ our Lord'. On the reverse side is a soldier's prayer that reads: 'O Lord, thou knowest how busy I must be this day. If I forget thee, do not thou forget me.' This was the prayer of Sir Jacob Astley, before the Battle of Edgehill in 1642.

Note also a soldier's prayer sent to the Regiment on 13 February 1991 by E G Beckerley of Rushden, Northants, a tank driver in a Yeomanry Regiment during the Second World War, and again during the Korean War as an 8th Hussar. [The 4th and 8th Hussars were amalgamated in 1958 to form The Queen's Royal Irish Hussars.] The prayer was found at El Agheila in December 1941 and quoted by Field Marshal Montgomery before the Allied attack on the Rhine in 1945. By an unknown author, it reads;

> I'm but the man my mother bore,
> A simple man and nothing more,
> But - God of strength and gentleness,
> Be pleased to make me nothing less.
> Help me, again, when death is near,
> To mock the haggard face of fear,
> That when I fall - if fall I must -
> My soul shall triumph in the dust.

Egyptian Divisions will advance 24 hours early, that is tomorrow. Two more packets of NAPS per man to be issued. Last outgoing post 0800hrs tomorrow. Burial is a sub-unit responsibility. Burials are unlikely to take place until we reach the reconstitution line. The procedure is that we go back to collect the dead. Bodies are to be placed in sleeping bags and then buried beside their vehicles. Authority has been granted for temporary burial on Saudi soil. Bodies will also be buried temporarily in Iraq but recovered to the United Kingdom in due course. Enemy in 1st (BR) Division area in essence four brigades. Iraqi 48 Infantry Division is expected to be mopped up by US forces, specifically 1 Infantry Division. 1st (BR) Division to be at Phase Line SMASH in 48 hours.[30]

Dawn. Have just got up. I am in the Warrior. Captain Richard Bryson the FOO is also here and, like me, writing a letter. Once 'stand to' is finished, we wash and have breakfast and then to the daily 'O' Group at 0830. This is how it's been since I have been here. In many ways it seems like a lifetime. I expect you think so too. By the time this arrives, that routine will have gone because we too will have gone. You will know where we are and what we are doing.

Captain Johnny Ormerod [QRIH] keeps us amused with tremendous stories. This is the gist of one of them: the subject was a five-month riding course in Italy. Johnny was based outside Rome and had the time of his life. He schooled in the morning and played polo in the afternoon.[31] The Italians produced a most impressive-looking training programme. Of course the programme never worked. Day one involved something to do with what Johnny took to be some form of equestrian PT. He arrived punctually at the gymnasium, having pushed aside the cobwebs to get in. Half an hour later an Italian officer turned up in sparkling riding kit, clicked his heels and inquired, 'Cappuccino?' And so it went from there. Imagine being based outside Rome for five months. With occasional forays to Florence - the Uffizi, the Pazzi Chapel, the monastery of San Marco.[32]

I seem to have been writing for ages saying one more letter. This is almost my last because we go tomorrow. I am in the Warrior with the other members of the crew all scribbling away too. That in itself is a reassurance, an action that indicates the nature of the game. In essence, Comradeship with a capital C. So I am amongst friends. I have known this crew three days. Circumstances are such that I have got to know them better in that time than I would normally have done in a year. In a matter of hours we will be in the thick of the fighting. We expect to fight for ten days. We are very comforted by the support we have from every quarter but, when it comes to the cold reality of locking with the enemy, there is no feeling of glamour. Just apprehension and the nagging worry about not letting others down. Of course I have no burden of responsibility to bear. All I am doing is sharing the risk.

[Letter to Mrs A E M Watt] *It's dawn. I am writing this in the back of a Warrior which is now my home with B Squadron QRIH. I am in the same vehicle as the Forward Observation Officer, Captain Richard Bryson. The crew are superb. In our last Concentration Area we went through the full range of emotions presumably anyone going into a full-scale set-piece battle always goes through. My father must have had exactly the same doubts and fears as myself. I never want to do this again! But we are near the border now and all that is behind us. We want to go and finish the job. I think the Iraqi army will break and I hope very soon. Although enormous in size, I sense it is fairly near total collapse. It just needs a short and extremely violent jolt to break it completely. Writing this section later in the day. We go in shortly. This is my last chance to write a note to you.*

Sunday 24 February: The First Day (G Day) An auspicious day. Dawn broke with a fierce wind and driving rain. As the 'O' Group huddled together, Colonel Denaro opened 'Prayers' with the observation that, when the 8th Hussars advanced at El Alamein, it was also pouring with rain. A very large minefield, measuring 100 kilometres square, has been located to the

Regimental Orders Group, the CO's briefing, 24 February 1991

north, apparently designed to protect the Tawakkulna Division. The Americans have laid scatterable mines in the 1st (BR) Division area. Mines fired by MLRS [Multiple Launch Rocket System] and timed to explode on 28 February.

Casualties: if casualties are light in Iraq, bodies will not be buried, but will be recovered to a Brigade RV. They will then be dealt with by the War Graves Commission and taken back to Saudi Arabia.

Points from Commanding Officer with words to this effect;

> 'Remember we will be in enemy territory. Crews must not stray from vehicles on foot at any time and never forget the danger of mines. Vehicles must not bunch. A2 Echelon [supporting vehicles and troops] must zig-zag, not leaguer in neat lines. For tank squadrons, the main thing to remember is to keep going whatever the task, and be aggressive to minimize casualties'. Colonel Denaro's final words were 'The best of luck and God bless'. Major Nigel Beer, the leader of C Squadron, from this point onwards under the command of 1 Staffords, was heard to say 'See you on SMASH' (Phase Line SMASH). There was much hand-shaking as officers and men wished each other *'Bonne chance'* and then quickly dispersed.[33]

Situation Report, G Day: Overview French half-way to their objective, WHITE; 101 Airborne have secured their primary objective, COBRA; 1 Infantry Division have taken 1,000 POWs. Joint Northern Command have made two breaches but will not exploit until tomorrow (G+1). The MEF [Marine Expeditionary Force] has advanced 30 kilometres into Kuwait, 3,000 POWs taken. Iraqi counter-attack in progress against Task Force RIPPER (MEF). One Iraqi POW 'surrendering' to MEF with a claymore mine attached to his body, blew himself up, killing a number of US Marines. Battle Group Orders issued at 1600 on G Day in the Staging Area.

A final note. This will be old news to you, and when you receive this letter, we will be on our way. [President] Bush has just announced the ground offensive. All night aircraft flew over in unprecedented numbers, and the thud of explosions rumbled along the border area. Now dawn. We are starting to get ourselves together for a move. We have received orders, objectives, timings, etc. The media will no doubt keep you informed of every move the Allies make! I intend to draw all the time while the war is on. This is the most important time. I must draw when I least feel like it, to record the essence of what it is like in the front line. That is where I need to be. Glad when this is all over. I promise to settle down after this show!!

Sketched Major David Swann's tank *Belfast*. The tank was side on, facing left. The crew's bivvy was still up. The gun was traversed over the side while the crew checked the oil levels. Notes in my sketch-book read 'very strong wind from the south blowing right to left'. To the left was the FOO's Warrior. In the foreground was David Swann's 9 x 9 tent. In the immediate foreground was a pile of compo boxes and some eggs 'with a sheet over the top flapping wildly in the wind'. Crews were busy packing up in preparation for the move to a Battle Group leaguer and, in turn, to the Staging Area. Once in the Staging Area I managed two more sketches. The first recorded B Squadron formed up in 'lane 3 of the Staging Area before launching breakout operations onto Line SMASH, via intermediate Objective, ZINC'. The sketch was 'scribbled in the dark'. I noted that Johnny Ormerod's tank *Ballyjamesduff*, call sign 0C, had its gun traversed right to the 3 o'clock position to allow access to the engine. 'The squadron fitters and the driver of 0C [call sign *Zero Charlie*], Trooper Winn, worked all night to get this tank fit for battle. The problem was a connecting pipe in the Auxiliary Power Unit which has perished' I also noted that 'at 2230 MLRS could be seen beyond the far column of tanks launching above the horizon like fireworks and apparently moving in slow motion'. The second sketch recorded Major David Swann's 'O' Group at 2300hrs. 'Orders were given in a rapidly assembled 9 x 9 tent. Very little light. Only the light of troop leaders' torches'. The map was set up on the far wall of the 9 x 9. The metal bar that supported the apex of the tent was 'just visible'. The 'shadows of figures were reflected on the canvas roof'. In the foreground 'two troop leaders stood hunched over notebooks taking orders for the Irish Hussars attack on Objective ZINC, *en route* to Line SMASH'.

'The Fitters'. Working to repair *Ballyjamesduff*, 24 February 1991

Captain Johnny Ormerod, Second-in-Command B Squadron QRIH, recorded the activities on G Day as follows;

> 'At 0200 the 1st Infantry Division, "The Big Red One" of the US VII Corps, crossed the Iraqi border, seizing a bridgehead as far as Phase Line NEW JERSEY by 2359 that day. Shortly after 1400 hours the Squadron moved off to the Regimental Staging Area... We had practised this procedure on numerous occasions and for many it was difficult to imagine it was the Real Thing! The transporters failed to materialize, presumably because everything was brought forward so quickly, and after a series of rapid briefings we moved up to the Forward Staging Area on tracks, arriving there about 1700 hours... At this stage we were unsure as to when we were going to move and were relieved to eventually hear that we would get a full night's sleep...

Monday 25 February: The Second Day (G+1) Battle Group Orders were given at 0745 hours in the Forward Staging Area. Began advance to FUP from Staging Area at 1005hrs. Report of Americans (1 Infantry Division) finding a minefield and a 500-pound unexploded bomb. 1101hrs: report that enemy had moved into a counter-penetration position on intended Blue [Allied] objective on Line SMASH, which turned out not to be true. 1215: B Squadron QRIH crossed from Saudi Arabia into Iraq on Phase Line VERMONT, the 'Border Berm'. Advanced from FUP at 1525. At 1615 the FOO's Warrior (call sign 13) put down speculative fire on suspected enemy positions with the 7.62mm chain gun. So too did the tanks of B Squadron, using main armament. At 2040 QRIH reached Line BURT.[34]

I made four sketches at this time: the first recorded the Commanding Officer's 'O' Group at 0745. Helmeted figures huddled round the seated figure of Colonel Arthur Denaro 'with a map across his knees'. To his left was the crouched figure of the Operations Officer, Captain Robert Hutton, who had already given his section of the orders, wearing an American parka. To his right was the Adjutant, Captain Andrew Cuthbert, wearing a flak jacket and a regimental pattern, desert-coloured Guernsey with the 'Desert Rat' insignia on the right arm, scribbling notes, standing braced against the open door of the APC. The second sketch showed Major David Swann's 'O' Group rapidly assembled at 0800hrs. The officers formed a semicircle beside his tank, *Belfast*. Most sat on the sand. David Swann knelt 'with a notebook in his right hand and his map across his knees', having quickly marked his map with the key information from Battle Group orders. The ground was dotted with clumps of camel-thorn showing silvery against the red-ochre of the desert. The third sketch depicted the front view of *Ballyjamesduff* during a halt, with the gun traversed right, 'two kilometres south of the Iraqi border', sketched from the FOO's Warrior. The final sketch that day recorded B Squadron in FUP 'Blue' about to advance to Objective ZINC at 1510hrs. The foreground was formed by the rear wing of the FOO's Warrior with a bergen, two water cans, and a drum of cable slung from its side armour, *Belfast* in the middle distance and a second tank on the horizon. I noted that the sky was 'very dark grey'. I also noted that, 'at 1505hrs the Tawakkulna Republican Guard was hit hard by an Allied air strike', and we had the first sighting of POWs being escorted by the Irish Hussars at 1512hrs.

At 1540hrs, with some difficulty as I was bumping around in the back of the Warrior, I made some colour notes in my sketch-book, while advancing to contact towards Objective ZINC. The sky was pale blue-grey, the sand was grey-ochre, but red-ochre where the surface had been churned by tank tracks. It was of the utmost importance that the myriad elements of 1st (BR) Division followed the correct route from the Staging Area, through the minefield breach to the FUP. Each route and each FUP was identified by a colour. QRIH were assigned to route 'Blue' and FUP 'Blue', hence the jingle invented by Captain Nick Marshallsay, 2nd Royal Tank Regiment, to jog our memories; 'Pink is punk and Blue is true!'

Major David Swann's Orders Group,
25 February 1991

The timetable for the move of the QRIH into Iraq on G+1 was recorded in the Regimental War Diary as follows; 'At 0640, Regiment placed at 5 minutes NTM [notice to move] from 0830. Regimental Orders Group 0745. At this stage it was assessed that the Iraqis would fight and that they were deliberately giving ground to lure the Allied Forces into their killing zones. By 1400 hours the Regiment was firm in FUP Blue in Iraq. At 1507 the Regiment was ordered forward. It could have been an exercise, the troops and squadrons urged on by the Commanding Officer and moving in textbook fashion with little idea of what lay ahead... At 1909 the Regiment was ordered forward to Line BURT to provide direct fire support for 1 Staffords/Scots DG attack north-south through Objective ZINC. The Regiment was firm by 2020 hours. The weather was atrocious. Pitch black and cold with heavy rain. At 2220 hours artillery was heard to the south and rear. The Scots DG were attacking an Iraqi communications position.

Captain Tim Purbrick, commanding 4 Troop D Squadron QRIH, described the advance into Iraq in these words;

'At around 10.30 am on the 25th February G+1, D Squadron QRIH led the 44 tanks of the Battle Group out of Staging Area 3, and we drove 40 kilometres into Iraq and the bridgehead made by 1 (US) Infantry Division. In FUP Blue we shook out in preparation for taking up the advance. The SQMS [Squadron Quartermaster-Sergeant] fuel truck gave most tanks a squirt of diesel. Two kilometres later we took up the advance from the Americans, not only for the Irish Hussars, but also for 7th Armoured Brigade, 1st (BR) Division, and VII (US) Corps. The ground was rolling desert with scrubby bushes and overcast skies, but no enemy so far. As night came on, rain rolled in and our thermal pictures degraded such that we could just about make out the tank in front, and it was only due to satellite navigation systems that we could maintain any kind of movement.

Tuesday 26 February: The Third Day (G+2) 2 and 40 Field Regiments and the General Support Group which includes MLRS opened up on nine targets on Objective ZINC from 0100 to 0119hrs, that is, 48 guns at 30 rounds per gun which totals 1440 rounds in 19 minutes. The din was tremendous and the ground shook. Flashes could be seen at the gun and target end. It pelted with rain. At 0150 1 Staffords, QRIH, and Scots DG Battle Groups moved onto Objective ZINC, with QRIH Battle Group in the centre. Earlier Scots DG were involved in a fire-fight in which half a dozen tanks and other vehicles were destroyed. The squadrons of QRIH moved all together looking for hot spots with TOGS [Thermal Observation and Gunnery Sight]. Once a target was found, tanks used fire-and-manoeuvre. The weather overnight was appalling. Cold with drenching rain. From 0500-0600 B Squadron tried to track a column of enemy vehicles using TOGS, seen at extreme range. 4th Troop leader, Lieutenant Tim Buxton 17/21L, reported that he had run over a scatterable mine. It turned out to be an MLRS bomblet which caused no harm to his tank. Later Major David Swann's tank *Belfast* ran over another MLRS bomblet, which punctured the external fuel drums on the back of his tank, releasing all the extra fuel.

At 0620 B Squadron moved forward to examine an enemy position just short of Phase Line LAVENDER. At this stage POWs began to appear in order to surrender. Some were very badly injured and peppered with bomblet rounds. Others died from wounds later, to add to the eight dead already in this position. B Squadron moved onto Line LAVENDER. Two or three vehicles were destroyed by Challenger, including a BRDM [Russian-built Iraqi reconnaissance vehicle]. At 0720 three or four men were seen in trenches. At 0724 a B Squadron tank knocked out a T55 [Russian-built Iraqi tank] with two rounds of HESH [High Explosive Squash Head ammunition]. At 0738 five enemy vehicles were seen moving south. A number of tanks were destroyed, including three T55s, one of which was destroyed by Captain Johnny Ormerod and his gunner Trooper Cater [17/21L], in *Ballyjamesduff*. At 0752 approx 30 Iraqis surrendered, and a number of tanks were engaged. At 0809 another group of 40 Iraqis surrendered to QRIH Battle Group. My overriding impressions that night were twofold: firstly, the professionalism shown in taking on the enemy, that is, the calmness in identifying and destroying those who presented a threat, combined with the restraint and humanity shown to those who did not; secondly, the devastating effect of artillery at night.

Belfast manoeuvres on Objective ZINC, 26 February 1991

Captain Tim Purbrick [17/21L], commanding 4 Troop D Squadron QRIH, described the battle for Objective ZINC as follows;

'By midnight we'd come 100 kilometres and up against the edge of an enemy position codenamed ZINC - it could have been the 12th Armoured Division of the Iraqi army, but real-time intelligence couldn't help us with exactly what was in front of us. So at 0115 (26 February) a 19-minute artillery and MLRS strike began to soften up the enemy. When the barrage lifted we pushed forward gingerly about two kilometres, where we began to dig in for the night. Half an hour later, numerous heat sources began to appear on our thermal pictures, moving from north to south across the rear of the enemy position before vanishing eastwards. D Squadron moved forward to engage this opportunity target, which was assessed to be tanks and trucks withdrawing. At the end of the short battle, ten or so enemy vehicles had been destroyed by a mixture of fin [armour piercing] anti- tank rounds and HESH explosive rounds. As dawn came up half an hour later, we began to see T55 tanks, hull down, pointing towards us. Our initial engagement began with HESH, which we had loaded for our night battle. The first round fell short, showering the

'The Battle for ZINC'. Challengers engage Iraqi armour, 26 February 1991

enemy tank with sand and shrapnel. We loaded fin and this round went into the berm behind which the tank was hiding, whilst the third and final round entered the glacis plate and exited through the gearbox at the rear, igniting its bomb load and destroying the tank at a range of 3,600 metres. A few minutes later we took on an unidentified vehicle at 4,700 metres - two-and-a-half miles away - scoring a first round hit, causing the vehicle to explode in a massive fireball. It continued to burn for the next hour. Our first 24 hours at war had seen us advance 100 kilometres into enemy territory, surprising the Iraqis - and ourselves - with our speed and ability to bring down fire accurately to destroy enemy vehicles, whilst remaining invisible to him and beyond his maximum engagement ranges.

Lieutenant Will Wyatt 17/21L, attached to C Squadron QRIH, made the following observations on this phase of the battle;

'We had little involvement in the actual night battle for Objective ZINC but took a staggering number of prisoners, which surprised us more than it did them, as we didn't have to fire a single shot. It proved a good way to break ourselves into the oddities of war and was certainly a better first contact than it could otherwise have been! We also had an amazing view of the battle slightly further south, certainly the best fireworks display any of us will ever see! The night skies were lit by a continuous pounding of the MLRS and the flashes of tanks engaging.

Lieutenant Tim Buxton 17/21L, attached to B Squadron QRIH, described the advance to Objective PLATINUM as follows;

'From Objective ZINC we advanced toward Objective PLATINUM 1, a regimental-sized enemy position, with our own Lynx helicopters firing missiles over our heads combined with artillery. The sky was clear, but a vicious wind was whipping the sand up to about the level of the gunner's sight, making the visibility poor. We stopped approximately 2.5 kilometres short of the objective and engaged the enemy. 4th Troop saw most of the enemy [the Troop destroyed four Iraqi tanks]... The Troop then pushed 600 metres further forward, in front of the Squadron, to look for depth positions. We then went into PLATINUM 2, where the Irish Hussars were the Brigade's fire support. Little resistance was put up, as the Iraqis had diverted some hours earlier. We then moved north, halting just south of Line SMASH. Here we re-supplied with fuel and ammo and had a few hours' sleep. All the drivers got out of their cabs for the first time in two days.

Some observations made by Captain Tony Hood on the Iraqi casualties and prisoners of war encountered by B Squadron, on the night of the MLRS bombardment on Objectives ZINC and PLATINUM, were as follows;

'Eight dead, 14 injured. Of the 14, three died later from severe injuries caused by bomblets from MLRS. Their bodies were peppered with shrapnel wounds. One of those who died had lost an eye which was hanging from its socket. The uninjured element of this group

A burning Iraqi T55 tank on Objective ZINC, 26 February 1991

had made no attempt to administer first aid to their fellows. This may have been in keeping with the Iraqi policy of treating their wounded after, but not during, battles. Consequently some soldiers had simply bled to death, to which they seem resigned on the basis of the 'Will of Allah'. Some soldiers were warmly clothed in three or four layers of clothing. Others were thinly clothed and some had no shoes. Whether well clothed or not, those who became casualties were soaked through with rainwater or blood. On the night of the bombardment on Objective ZINC the weather was utterly filthy, with heavy rain driven on a high wind.

The crew of *Ballyjamesduff* wash during a brief pause in the fighting, 26 February 1991

'The following day 22 enemy surrendered to B Squadron QRIH during the attack on PLATINUM 2. The group came forward carrying a large white flag held horizontally by its corners, parallel to the ground; a pathetic sight. The white flag was a parachute from a British para illuminating round. Three or four Iraqis could speak English. All were strongly against Saddam Hussein and were delighted to have become POWs. Four of this group had no shoes. They had plenty of cigarettes but no lighters. They were delighted with boiled sweets and matches from our compo rations. One Iraqi doctor reported that he had not washed or changed his clothes for 40 days and the shortage of water was so severe that soldiers were reduced to drinking IV drips. Iraqi POWs seemed very grateful for the first aid given to them and for the compassion shown by British forces. After an Allied attack elsewhere a group of five Iraqis surrendered. It was this group who reported that three Iraqi battalions wished to surrender. And so they did. That night the BBC World Service announced that 26 Iraqi divisions had been destroyed or rendered non-operational, with 30,000 Iraqi POWs taken.

I made three sketches that day (G+3). The first, drawn at 0545 hours, depicted the half-seen profile of *Belfast* emerging from the inky blackness of dawn with 'The Queen's Royal Irish Hussars preparing to strike into Kuwait against the Republican Guard'. The second was drawn from the back of the FOO's Warrior, 'an unfinished sketch of *Ballyjamesduff* on a ridgeline beside an observation tower at 1140 hours during the advance from Iraq into Kuwait'. I noted that '...the sky was blue-grey, the scrub was sage green and the sand was ginger-coloured in the light areas, run through with darker patches of green-grey'. The third sketch showed the rear left wing of the FOO's Warrior and *Ballyjamesduff* on a ridge. A further note read as follows;

> '...overnight 27 February the Americans captured Kuwait City. Thirty-three thousand POWs taken so far. A battle rages to the north of the position shown in the sketch. The position is the start line for the advance north to destroy the tank reserves of the Republican Guard, which is trapped between Kuwait City and the position taken by the US Airborne Corps [Objective COBRA, taken by 101 (US) Air Assault Division].'

I later made another three sketches. The first, at 0809, showed 'the surrender of about 23 POWs to B Squadron QRIH on Phase Line LAVENDER, beyond Objective ZINC' with B Squadron Battle Captain, Captain Tony Hood, moving forward in his Warrior to tend possible casualties, the FOO's Warrior in the foreground, and *Belfast* in the middle distance. I noted that the grey sky became increasingly dark at the time. I also recorded the roar of Apache helicopters on the ridge to the west. I made a supplementary note that the commander of the group of POWs depicted was a full colonel and that 'many commanders had cut and run'. On the night preceding the attack on Objective ZINC, Iraqi officers had ordered their men to stay in trenches and to emerge in the morning after the Allied artillery bombardment. In fact, most of the officers ran during the night in vehicles earmarked for that purpose.

I then made a hurried sketch of *Belfast* before the Regiment moved up to a fire support position for the attack on PLATINUM 1 and PLATINUM 2, 'standing up in a buffeting wind with spitting rain and driven sand'. It was indeed 'dirty weather with a cold blustery wind'. Finally, at 1645hrs, I sketched 'the view from the FOO's Warrior with its back doors open with a Challenger passing from left to right'. I noted that we were 'about to move east to the Limit of Exploitation, Phase Line SMASH' and that 'contact with the Iraqi tactical and operational reserve is expected'. The crew of the FOO's Warrior were Lance-Bombardier Mills from Burton-on-Trent, Staffordshire, of B Battery 1 RHA, attached to 40 Field Regiment; Bombardier Kingscott from Scunthorpe, Humberside; and the driver, Gunner Ashton, (known as 'Ash') from Nottingham.

Wednesday 27 February: The Fourth Day (G+3) I awoke with a start in the early hours to the brilliant glare of an electric storm. The whole sky was lit up. As I came to my senses I suddenly realized that this was no storm, but a full-scale artillery attack by MLRS engaged in a deadly display of firepower, pounding Iraqi positions to our north. It was difficult to establish the exact position of the launchers as salvo after salvo of rockets streaked into the night, each rocket cutting an illuminated path and casting residual light over many kilometres of the battlefield. We gazed in silence, and could only be thankful that such ferocity had not been unleashed on us. The launchers fell silent but MLRS were to be in action several more times before dawn. We 'stood to' at 0545, after which we received orders from B Squadron leader Major David Swann, who held his 'O' Group huddled round the dozer blade of Johnny Ormerod's tank *Ballyjamesduff*. VII (US) Corps was to advance north east astride the Wadi Al Batin destroying all enemy. Thrust to end north-west of Kuwait City. 1st (BR) Division was to advance east to Objective VARSITY. Order of March, arrowhead: A Squadron leading, D north, B south. Advance ordered at 0744, with B Squadron now designated point in the Battle Group layout. A tank ran over an unexploded cluster bomb, but it had no effect on the tracks. At 0820 B Squadron leader's tank broke down. B Squadron Second-in-Command, Captain Johnny Ormerod, took over temporarily as Squadron leader. Large number of bomblets reported in area of all enemy positions. 0925, B Squadron reached Iraq-Kuwait border, having brushed aside light opposition. 0950, lead troops reported white flags on enemy positions. 0952, report of mines seen to south. Initial impression of Kuwait: much more vegetation in the form of camel-thorn. Plants sage green, but interspersed with a few smaller, darker plants. The reddish sand was run through with darker, greyer streaks and patches. Between 1030 and 1100, B Squadron negotiated a very large quarry area where tanks without TRIMBLE [the satellite navigation equipment] had difficulty with navigation. Once clear, the Squadron advanced across a level plain. 1107 Scots DG in contact to the north.

At 1119 a tragic 'Blue on Blue' incident occurred, in which two QRIH reconnaissance vehicles were engaged in error by secondary and main armament from an American M1 tank.[35] The two injured soldiers were Lance-Corporal Balmforth, who sustained a head wound and Lance-Corporal Lynch, who sustained a shrapnel wound to the thigh. B Squadron occupied a Start Line east of Wadi Al Batin, facing north, parallel with Iraq-Kuwait border. No move before 1800. Anticipated that 1st (BR) Division will move north to destroy Republican Guard, which is reported to have been trapped by the [US] 82nd Airborne Division to the north-west in Iraq. At this stage I transferred from the FOO's Warrior to another, commanded by Captain Tony Hood, B Squadron Battle Captain. His main task is to lead the two Squadron ambulances from A to B on the battlefield, to supervise the casevac chain, including reporting of casualties and the burial of dead, Allied and enemy.

Captain Johnny Ormerod recorded the actions of B Squadron QRIH on G+3 as follows;

'It was at 0400hrs that the Squadron got the first hint of the task that lay ahead... Orders came: we were to advance into Kuwait to seize Objective VARSITY. The Regiment was rear left in the Brigade and the Squadron was rear right in the Regiment. We were to move as soon as possible. We took up our normal leaguer formation and got moving very quickly. B Squadron was instructed by the Colonel to take over as point squadron. We crossed the Start Line on time, broke into advance formation, married up with the Scots DG and headed for the Kuwait border. To our front there were large groups of Iraqis and many more appearing out of the mist. The Squadron continued with Lieutenant Buxton in front as the TRIMBLE tank... At about 0700 we led the Regiment into Kuwait across the Wadi al Batin... We approached an area of rough ground around a quarry, quickly named 'moon country'. Troops were split to the four winds as they searched for a route through. In retrospect, had this been a defensive position we could have suffered badly... We continued to Objective VARSITY which was unoccupied... For the first time we became aware of the burning oil-fields, the dark grey skies producing an eerie combination with the orange sand. For many crews it was the first opportunity to listen to the World Service and discover quite how devastating the operation had been... Rumours of future operations were rife. We were all desperately enthusiastic to close with the Republican Guard and have a crack at a T72 [tank]. The warning order that day suggested we would sweep up the Kuwait/Iraq border to the Republican Guard, the limit of exploitation being the Euphrates, an exciting possibility which unfortunately was not to happen... The Squadron adopted its night-time routine. The World Service broadcast the possibility of a ceasefire which was met with mixed emotions.

Thursday 28 February: The Fifth Day (G+4) During the night of G+3 there was talk of a ceasefire. At 0600 QRIH ordered to move due east 30 kilometres to blocking position. Task: to cut the Basra road north of Kuwait City on Line LANCE within Objective COBALT. Challengers thundered forward. At 0647 saw an abandoned ZSU 23/4 [Russian-built Iraqi self-propelled anti-aircraft gun] on a road. At 0725 B Squadron reached Objective COBALT. We received warnings of chemical anti-personnel mines and anti-tank mines. One tank crew saw a dog trigger a mine during the approach to the objective.

The War Diary of the QRIH covering the final advance to Objective COBALT reads as follows;

'At 0424hrs Brigade issued orders. The ceasefire would be delayed from 0500 to 0800hrs. The Brigade H hour to advance on Objective COBALT, the Basra Road, was set for 0630hrs. At 0509hrs RHQ ordered the Regiment to pack up and be ready to move at any time. At 0600hrs the Regiment moved, B Squadron leading, A Squadron left and D

Squadron right. The Regiment was to charge, destroying all enemy *en route*. At COBALT the Regiment was to secure the area and cut off the Iraqi retreaton the Basra Road. The weather was overcast, the smog from the oil fires blackening the sky and a thick fog had rolled in, reducing visibility to 400 metres or less. The Regiment had covered over 40 kilometres in bad visibility at terrific speed. It had arrived at the Basra Road and seen the devastating effect of modern air power. The road was littered with destroyed vehicles, both military and civilian. It was an apocalyptic sight.

Major Nigel Beer, C Squadron leader QRIH, said later; 'If the advance to Objective VARSITY could be described as a canter, the advance to Objective COBALT was a gallop.'

Captain Johnny Ormerod described the final hours of Operation DESERT SABRE with words to this effect;

'The Gunners produced the goods again and gave us a sneak preview of the day's tasks with a report from Brigade. The Euphrates was out and instead it was going to be best speed to the Kuwait City/Basra road to Objective COBALT. There was a limiting factor - the ceasefire would take effect at 0800. If we were to achieve anything, we would have to reach there before then. The Iraqis had been withdrawing rapidly from Kuwait City and we hoped to cut off their retreat. By the time orders came through from the Regiment our maps were marked and the Squadron had a pretty good idea of what was going on, so we were able to react very quickly. The Regiment was to be the point Battle Group of the Brigade, and the Squadron the point of the Regiment. Speed of movement was of paramount importance. We were given 15 minutes to get going across the Start Line. As orders were being relayed, the Squadron instinctively moved into its leaguer formation and began to advance. Things happened so quickly that it was in fact only after we had

Orders Group, Kuwait, shortly before the advance to Objective
COBALT, dawn, 28 February 1991

crossed the Start Line that the full details of our task were passed down. We covered 45 kilometres in the first hour... The satellites went down for a short period of time and we quickly reverted to the compass which worked remarkably well.

'It was a good morning for the Squadron. At one point we were nine kilometres ahead of the Regiment! In different circumstances this might have been rather risky, but the race was on and the Colonel was just behind us... The Squadron advanced to the road. It was a miserable but memorable sight. A deserted motorway with destroyed and abandoned military vehicles scattered about. Early sightings by 1st Troop reported tanks on transporters withdrawing; however, as we closed, it became obvious that they had already been destroyed. There were no signs of a retreating army but, in retrospect, the carnage of the Mutla Ridge to our south may well have prevented that retreat. The Squadron crossed the road and took up defensive positions facing east... There was much concern about the possibility of anti-personnel mines around our vehicles, so for the time being crews remained mounted. At 0800 the ceasefire came into effect. Guns were cleared and brews were made as we awaited further orders... The Squadron had driven some 300 kilometres since entering southern Iraq and by-passed or engaged elements of between four and five Iraqi divisions. This was a major achievement, although we were frustrated at not having met the Republican Guard... However, we were luckier than they. We were all still in one piece.

Elements of 7th Armoured Brigade later reported moving through abandoned enemy positions that were vast in size. For example, Objective COPPER measured approximately 35 kilometres by 30 kilometres. In Iraq, Allied policy has been to destroy equipment that the enemy could recover and use again. Once in Kuwait, Iraqi equipment was left intact if possible.

At this stage Captain Tony Hood provided more details on the plight of the enemy on Objective ZINC the night of 26 February. 'The soldier who had lost an eye also had a hole the size of a golf ball in the back of his skull. We managed to get a drip into him but sadly he died later.' Another Iraqi soldier, with a broken wrist, 'sat cross-legged not two yards from him' but much to Captain Hood's amazement 'made no attempt to aid his critically-injured comrade'. Injuries varied from 'loss of limbs to large flesh tears, to soldiers riddled with small puncture wounds all over their bodies. These were difficult to treat but the internal injuries were the main problem.' The problem of treating the Iraqi wounded was compounded by the '...number of MLRS bomblets scattered on the ground. It was extremely hazardous skipping between the bomblets trying to give first aid to the wounded.' Later the psyops teams were very useful in bringing in 'a group of 22 prisoners assisted by a Saudi officer screaming down a loudspeaker'. At the same time;

    'Four more POWs surrendered to Staff Sergeant Griffin of 4th Troop. They were sent back along the axis as we had no time to move them ourselves. They walked for a while but, having failed to find any Allied tanks, returned to give themselves up again. We then loaded them onto the Warrior and drove back to the Battle Group POW cage. They said they were thirsty so we gave them water... They then ran off happily to their comrades in the POW cage. The doctor we found was very well-spoken. He told us he had been pulled out of his civilian practice in Baghdad five months before the war. He was put into the front line without any supplies to look after 800 men. Dysentery was rife but he had no drugs to control it. He had not washed for three months and water had run out eight days before the Allied offensive. They were reduced to drinking IV drips.

For his work with the wounded Captain Tony Hood was Mentioned in Despatches.

1   The name of the Tawakkulna Division may derive from the Arabic word *tawakkul*, meaning 'trust'.

2   On clear days we would often see groups of B-52s flying in formation at very great altitude, far too high to make any sound. These huge aeroplanes appeared as tiny specks, each one leaving four white exhaust trails in its wake.

3   We longed for baths which, after a while, seemed to represent the pinnacle of civilization. One soldier told me how, when Operation GRANBY was over, he planned to lie in a bath with the plug out and hot water running all day.

4   1st (BR) Division was now part of VII (US) Corps. Concentration Area KEYES was named after Lieutenant-Colonel Geoffrey Keyes VC MC CG, who died leading the heroic raid on General Rommel's main headquarters at Beda Littoria in North Africa in 1941.

5   KKMC was created for an estimated 70,000 inhabitants as part of the Saudi defence plan. It lies near Hafar-al-Batin, a defensive base on the desolate plain that runs from the border with Iraq directly to Riyadh. Despite immense physical and logistical problems (the city lies over 400 kilometres from Riyadh and 375 kilometres from the port of Al Jubayl), work began in 1976, at a cost of 5.2 billion dollars.

6   After the war United Nations inspection teams hunted for nuclear, ballistic, biological and chemical weapons sites in Iraq, for destruction. The first unmistakeable documentary proof of Iraq's programme to build nuclear weapons was discovered on 23 September 1991, including information on trigger mechanisms for a nuclear device.

7   The author visited the Lebanon in more peaceful times, living at Shemlan in the stunningly attractive hills that overlook Beirut and swimming at the luxurious St George's Club in the centre of the capital. Once again man has contrived to reduce a gleaming city to a sterile shell.

8   The Kuwaiti island re-captured from the Iraqis on 24 January following an air-sea battle was Qaruh. The island lies 22 miles off the Kuwaiti coast and was thought to have been used by the Iraqis as a command post. Three Iraqi ships were sunk, one by an American A-6 Intruder aircraft, another by a Royal Navy Sea Skua anti-ship missile and a third by an Iraqi mine. Three Iraqis were killed and five were captured. Many prisoners were reported to be ill-fed, lice-infested or covered in sores.

9   Iraq began to pump millions of gallons of oil into the Gulf circa 25 January, probably to impede a possible Allied amphibious landing. The oil caused a slick measuring 30 miles by ten miles, containing about five to eight million barrels of oil, which came to rest

against the Saudi coast, penned in by the islands of Abu Ali, between Khafji in the north and Al Jubayl in the south. It threatened a region listed as a special area by the International Marine Organization because of its sensitive ecology. At risk were millions of shore and sea birds, including shearwaters, petrels, gulls, terns, grebes, and socotra cormorants, the latter being unique to Saudi Arabia. Bird deaths were estimated at 15,000-30,000. Also at risk were porpoises and dolphins, turtles, and fish. The desalination plants that provide Kuwait and Saudi Arabia with 90 per cent of their fresh water were also threatened. One year later, the effect of the oil slick on the inter-tidal zone was confirmed. This area of mangrove swamp and saltmarsh, essential for many fish and small animals such as shrimp and wading birds, had been largely wiped out.

[10] The Hammurabi Division was named after the King of Babylon, who ruled during the Second Millenium BC.

[11] On 29 January an Iraqi mechanized battalion with APCs and tanks crossed the border at Al Wafrah 50 miles north west of Khafji. The column attempted to trick the US Marines into thinking that they were defectors. The fighting lasted six hours and the Iraqis lost 22 tanks. The same day an Iraqi mechanized unit occupied Khafji. The Battle of Khafji lasted 37 hours. Saudi and Qatari troops killed 30 Iraqis and took 400 POWs.

[12] I was always most at ease when completely alone, away from the insistence of the human voice and the thump of generators. It was only then that I could fully absorb my surroundings: the patterns in the sand; the sculptures of camel-thorn; the shadows cast by the skeletons of camels half covered in drifting sand; or the tracks of lizards and jerboa. Sometimes there were flocks of larks, or kites wheeling, or eagles quartering. Once or twice I gathered stones so I could examine them later. There were small angular flints everywhere, whether we were in the deep, soft sand around Jubayl, or on the hard gravel plain leading north to Iraq and Kuwait. These opportunities were lost once we were on the move.

[13] The artist was born in 1947.

[14] An island in the Indian Ocean, used as a joint support facility by Britain and the USA.

[15] The Nebuchadnezzar Division was named after Nebuchadnezzar II, the most famous of the rulers of the Second Babylonian Empire. He is mentioned in the Bible as the conqueror of Palestine, the destroyer of the temple in Jerusalem in 597 BC and the ruler who brought to an end the independent Kingdom of Judah. The Medina Division was named after the oasis town 270 miles north of Mecca to which Muhammad and his followers went in AD622 to establish an *ummah* (community).

16   The tank was an FV4003 Centurion AVRE (Armoured Vehicle Royal Engineers) of 32 Armoured Engineer Regiment RE. This model is equipped with a demolition gun and is mainly used for the destruction of field fortifications and obstacles.

17   On 7 February 1991, three IRA mortar bombs were fired from a van parked in Whitehall. One of the bombs exploded in the garden of No. 10 Downing Street during a meeting of the War Cabinet, but there were no casualties.

18   The Adnan Division was named after the patriarch Adnan, who is by tradition one of the ancestors of the Arab race.

19   General Sir Peter de la Billière described the battle preparation phase of the Allied offensive with chilling simplicity; '...the ground war isn't going to start until we are satisfied the air operations have prepared the battlefield into the state we want it' (*Sunday Telegraph*, 3 March 1991). The value of precision guided weapons was proved conclusively in the Gulf War, virtually eliminating the traditional notion of a 3:1 superiority required by an attacking force. General de la Billière is reported to have said; 'I think precision bombing by the air force is something that many of us who are not airmen did not really believe. I believe it now.' The General went on to say that very few Iraqi troops had been found wounded, because most were killed in direct hits by precision bombing and shelling. The plan, according to Operations Director Brigadier-General Buster Glosson, was to defeat Iraq's air defences on the first day of the war using a variety of aircraft and Tomahawk missiles, and to have air superiority from then on. Special Forces, inserted into southern Iraq, were to lay laser target markers on anti-air radars, as A-10s, F-16s and F-15Es created a 'path' to Baghdad for F-117A Stealth fighters to hit command, control and communications centres.

20   These fears were well founded. One newspaper report, before the war, estimated that 50,000 Kurds or Iranians had been killed or injured by mustard, nerve or phosgene gas during the Iran-Iraq war of 1980-88. Another report stated that Iraq was in the process of developing biological weapons including bubonic plague, equine encephalitis, malaria, tularaemia, and West Nile fever (*Daily Telegraph*, 29 and 30 December 1990). During the strategic bombing phase, targets hit included the chemical and biological warfare plants at Samarra, Salman Pak, and Abu Gharib. It was fortunate indeed that the prevailing wind, which normally blows from north to south in the Gulf area in winter, suddenly changed direction quite by chance at this time, veering through 180 degrees during the Allied offensive. This was highly significant because it was these winds that would have borne these fearsome chemical or biological agents towards the Allies massed along the northern border of Saudi Arabia, had the Iraqis used them. That they did not do so may be attributed partly to the unfavourable wind direction, but also to the paralysis of their command and control system, their heavy losses of artillery and, I imagine, a tacit but

unmistakeable signal from the Americans at the highest political level that this would not be a sensible move.

After the war, a third newspaper report described how samples of some of the world's most deadly germ and chemical warfare substances were removed from Iraq's main chemical weapons factory at Samarra. It is understood the samples include Bis Sulfide mustard gas, Sarin and Tabun - two of the most toxic nerve gases. These disrupt the nervous system, causing convulsions and then paralysis. Death follows within minutes. A further batch of samples to be examined is likely to include agents for the spread of anthrax, botulism, cholera and encephalitis. The Iraqi government has told the UN that it has 30 chemical warheads for Scud missiles and 11,000 smaller chemical bombs and shells. Both Britain and the United States allege that Iraq has a far larger chemical arsenal. One report puts Iraq's store of mustard and nerve gas alone at circa 3,500 tons. Iraq does not admit to possession of any biological weapons (*Sunday Telegraph*, 23 June 1991).

By September 1991, UN officials had destroyed 8,000 Iraqi bombs, shells, and rockets, designed to be loaded with chemical agents. UN inspection teams also reported that Iraq had the capability to launch 30 Scud missiles fitted with chemical warheads. UK Foreign and Commonwealth Office experts estimate that it will take two years to destroy Iraq's chemical arsenal under UN Resolution 687.

[21] That evening I told the Commanding Officer Scots DG, Lieutenant-Colonel John Sharples, of my father's view of Iraq and his professional opinion of its army, drawn from his experiences while working with the British Military Mission to Iraq pre-1958. In essence a fascinating country with a friendly and likeable people, and a rotten army. Thirty years later my father's assessment of Iraq's military capability was still spot on!

[22] The Division moved to Assembly Area RAY between 14 and 16 February. RAY was similar to KEYES: flat, barren and featureless. The Division was now keen to finish the job. G Day, 'Go Day' [24 February] was awaited with growing impatience.

[23] Exercise DIBDIBAH CHARGE was the final confirmation that 1st (BR) Division was ready for action. The exercise also reflected the fact that the Division's role had changed. No longer was it our task to fight through the obstacle belt; that task now fell to the Americans. 1st (BR) Division's task would be to break out of an established bridgehead and destroy the enemy's tactical reserve.

[24] This meant that one aircraft took off every 33 seconds. At this stage it was estimated that more than 1,300 of the 4,000 tanks in KTO had been destroyed.

[25] The mission of 1 (US) Infantry Division was to create the breach into Iraqi territory.

That day the Division made 20 breaches of the border berm between Saudi Arabia and Iraq.

[26] According to a newspaper report Brigadier Cordingley had this to say of Iraq's leader; 'I think he doesn't fully understand the might of the Allied armies arrayed against him. But I suspect his military commanders do.' (*Sunday Telegraph*, 3 March 1991). Brigadier Cordingley also expressed his confidence in the Allied plan with the famous remark; 'I've got my skiing holiday booked for the first week in April and I'm bloody certain I'm going on it!'

[27] An entry in the QRIH War Diary reads as follows;
> 'The 22nd February was G-2. The Allies had been holding at G-3 for several days awaiting the outcome of the last-ditch diplomatic initiatives, and also to allow elements of the Allied land forces to get into their final positions. At last, after four months of deployment, after many expectations of war from November 1990 through to February 1991, after months of training, months of waiting, months of excitement and boredom, the mission was at last going to be executed. 24 February 1991 would be G Day.

[28] According to information gleaned from Iraqi POWs by Allied forces, morale in the rank-and-file of most divisions was shattered. As many as 100,000 men were reported to have deserted, many to the Shi'ite and Kurdish rebels. Fifty-five per cent of Iraq's 17 million population are Shi'ites and they provided most of the rank-and-file during the decade of expansion, in which Saddam expanded the army sixfold, an army which he could not possibly feed, clothe or equip efficiently. This inevitably led to poor morale caused primarily, according to an Iraqi field commander defector, Colonel Ahmed Al-Zaidi, by the political leadership which seeks to 'turn the army from an institution for defending the country into a tool to protect the regime'.

[29] Within VII (US) Corps the division of tasks was as follows: 1 (US) Infantry Division was to breach the obstacle belt in the Iraqi 48 Infantry Division area and then follow 1 and 3 (US) Armoured Divisions through the breach. 2 (US) Armoured Cavalry was to outflank 48 Infantry Division and initially protect the left flank of the breach. 1st (BR) Division was to pass through the breach and advance to destroy the Iraqi 12 Armoured Division (the main counter-attack force in the area), then be prepared to follow 1 and 3 (US) Armoured Divisions north to destroy the RGFC.

[30] 'Phase lines' were a series of map reference points used to assist the co-ordination and timing of the British advance.

[31] 4th Armoured Brigade and 7th Armoured Brigade played a long-awaited polo match

after the war at the Royal Berkshire Club on 16 July 1991, the result of a challenge thrown down in the Gulf. 4th Armoured Brigade won 4-1. The match was attended by General Sir Peter de la Billière and the prizes were presented by the Duchess of York.

[32]   My wife Jane and I visited Florence immediately after the Gulf War. We took great pleasure in visiting all these marvellous places but to me they hardly seemed real - the contrast was too abrupt.

[33]   At 0300 hours on G Day the ground offensive was launched. The French and Americans were pushing on and the bridgehead site was being pounded by artillery, B-52 bombers and Apache attack helicopters. The JFCN (Joint Force Command North, the Arab Force) prepared to attack the following day. 1st (BR) Division moved to a Staging Area 20 kilometres south of the obstacle belt.

[34]   Line BURT was named after Colonel Denaro's former home in Co. Donegal, Burt House, and his Jack Russell terrier.

[35]   The worst 'Blue on Blue' or 'Friendly Fire' incident occurred at 1500 hours on 26 February (G+2), when two Warrior vehicles of the 3rd Battalion, Royal Regiment of Fusiliers (part of 4th Armoured Brigade) were engaged in error by an American A-10 aircraft. There were 20 casualties, including nine dead.

CHAPTER FOUR
Aftermath

Thursday 28 February 1991: The Fifth Day (G + 4) Very murky weather and very poor visibility. An epic moment in the history of The Queen's Royal Irish Hussars as their tanks cut the Basra road. Challengers were half seen in strange early morning light in a blanket of grey cloud, tinged with faint traces of acid yellow. Clear evidence of the ecological disaster caused to the area by the burning oil wells. Two Challengers took up fire positions on the road itself. Others crossed the road moving in column and deployed to the east. Captain Tony Hood's Warrior halted at a road junction where a minor road joined the main highway. At that point there was an abandoned MTLB [Russian-built Iraqi armoured personnel carrier], an artillery piece, a T55 tank and some wrecked civilian vehicles.

Sketched a dead Iraqi soldier by the roadside. His left kneecap was missing and he had lost his right leg completely below the knee. Shattered bone protruded. His right boot was on its own, separated from the corpse. There was a gaping hole in his forehead; beneath the corpse the sand was bloodstained. Then sketched the remains of an articulated lorry or low loader which had been hit with colossal force - probably by an A-10. It was a tangle of wreckage, blown into thousands of tiny pieces. Beyond it was a British recce vehicle flying the Union Flag.

The Irish Hussars had set up their Headquarters on the Basra road. The Union Flag and the Regimental Flag flew from wireless masts in a stiff breeze. I finished my sketch of the dead Iraqi soldier, lying in the shallow dip that divided the Basra highway 400 yards south of Regimental Headquarters. As I knelt in the middle of the southbound lane, sketching the wrecked tank transporter, I suddenly heard the rumble of armour to the north. I completed as much of the sculpture of the wrecked transporter as I could. The faint rumble became a solid roar, as Challengers of the Scots Dragoon Guards emerged from the gloom that hung unshifting over the battlefield and thundered south toward Kuwait City.[1] A stirring sight, amidst the carnage and debris that littered the highway. Tanks roared past between wrecked vehicles, crunching through the debris scattered across the road surface and disappearing in a cloud of diesel exhaust and dust. Most flew the Scottish standard or the St Andrew's Cross from their wireless antennae, except in one case, the black and white Prussian eagle of a tank crew of the 14th/20th Hussars attached to the Scots DG. The expressions of the tank crews bore no sign of euphoria.

The Queen's Royal Irish Hussars' Headquarters on the Basra Road, 28 February 1991

A soldier escorted two POWs across the road towards the Headquarters of QRIH positioned in the dip between the north and southbound carriageways of the Basra road. Arms raised, they shuffled along, battleshocked. One of them limped. As I walked by the roadside, I was startled by a loud sharp report followed by a ricochet as an Allied scatterable mine self-destructed somewhere nearby. There were mines and bomblets littered everywhere.

Friday 1 March Dawn broke. We did not 'stand to'. Bliss. No helmets, flak jackets and weapons, or freezing cold staring into the blackness. Instead we lay in our sleeping bags and watched the sun come up. A clear warm day with a blue sky. As I lay beside the Warrior, I could see oil fires and a pylon line. Some of the pylons were leaning with the lines down. My main observation was the silence. No aeroplanes overhead, no distant thuds as bombs struck home, no roar of artillery or tanks. This constant background noise, sometimes slight, sometimes deafening, has been part of our lives for so long it has become normal. Today was different. We gazed across a grey gravel plain pitted with abandoned Iraqi bunkers. Plumes of smoke drifted on the horizon. The sun warmed our backs as we remained in our sleeping bags.

After breakfast we listened to the news on the World Service. General de la Billière was asked to comment. He replied with words to this effect; 'If I've got one message for the people at home today it is this: to get out there and ring your church bells, because this is one of the greatest victories that we've ever experienced, certainly in our lives and possibly in history'. He then went on to praise General Schwarzkopf for his dynamic leadership, and even his rudeness, which has 'got things done, and got them done so damned efficiently and enabled us to win this war'.

I then sped off to an abandoned Iraqi tank battalion position with about 30 tanks. The tanks were spread in a vast circle, each tank separated by about 600 metres. The diameter of the position was about a mile, the farthest tanks appearing as small indistinct specks. In the centre were command bunkers linked by land-line. Many tanks had received direct hits.[2] One tank had its turret blown off completely and dumped unceremoniously with its barrel stuck in the ground, muzzle first like a lance, some distance from the hull. The latter appeared to be intact but, on closer inspection, it became clear that the normally massively strong components of engine and gearbox had been reduced to tiny fragments. On the tanks and in the bunkers there was no sign of life; or death, except one body found in a bunker and another buried in a shallow grave marked by a wooden cross. Everywhere there were the signs of a fleeing broken army: gas masks, clothing, blankets; rotting food, mainly rice, dates, and flour; small arms, magazines, oil drums, wire cables, and boxes of ammunition.[3] Tank turrets had been shattered, distorted and filled to the brim with their own contents, now re-arranged and blackened by fire. Live ammunition of all types and calibres lay around; some loaded in machine guns, some still boxed. Tank rounds had broken away from ammunition racks and now protruded at odd angles from turrets. The tanks themselves seemed rather like ships out of control in heavy seas.

Iraqi T69 tanks destroyed by Allied air strikes on Objective COBALT, 1 March 1991

'Moonlight on the Battlefield'.
Abandoned Iraqi tank, Kuwait, 1 March 1991

Abandoned Iraqi bunker, Objective COBALT,
1 March 1991

Probably the most pathetic aspect was the sight of personal belongings scattered to the four winds. I found a child's jacket, bright pink in colour with a gold border round the pockets, and made in China. There seemed to be masses of boots, parkas, and coveralls, usually wrapped in plastic bags. Some of the Iraqi equipment seemed to be of medium quality, particularly the clothing. Other equipment was decidedly poor, for instance the NBC kit which consisted of a respirator of the most basic design and long yellow boots which reached to the knee. There were dozens of small individual chemical decontamination kits. The worst aspect was the NBC suit which consisted of a green rubber cape. It appeared to afford only limited protection and would have been a nightmare to fight in.

I saw a wrecked Italian Tornado in the centre of the tank battalion position, now in a thousand pieces and spread over an area about half a mile in diameter. I also saw the point of impact, a shallow elongated indentation about 20 yards in length. The tank positions were dug in behind berms with rocket screens forward. Some of the overhead cover to bunkers was flimsy. In other cases, bunkers were well constructed with overhead cover, consisting of corrugated iron, steel pickets, and concrete blocks covered with sand bags. Some bunkers had been hit, their contents blown everywhere: everything from coffee pots to cooking oil, from mattresses to sandals. There was silence except for the wind, which created swirls of sand; and pieces of paper which rustled as they sped through the position, catching here and there on the ground or against the stark silhouettes of tank hulks. A pack of feral dogs stole past in a long line, beating against the wind.[4] They were soon blurred by flurries of sand as they moved by. A wagtail settled for a moment in the lee of a bunker.

Oil well fires, Kuwait, early March 1991

Saturday 2 March Total British land battle casualties 19.[5] Total Iraqi dead estimated at about 80,000 at the time of writing.[6] Drew a sketch of *Ballybogey* flying the Union Flag, with a sleeping bag draped over the gun barrel to dry in the wind. Then a field petrol cooker. I looked north: a huge pall of smoke, many miles long, plumed from a fired oil well. The smoke completely blotted out the sun, which assumed the appearance of a pale orange moon, just one example among many of the ecological disasters inflicted on the Middle East by this monstrous Iraqi regime, adding yet another crime to its already heinous record. The journey from the Staging Area in Saudi Arabia to our final destination north-west of Kuwait City measured 359.3 kilometres (calculation by Fusilier Palmer, Royal Highland Fusiliers, driver of a Warrior of B Squadron QRIH).

[Letter to Mrs A E M Watt] *A short note to say I'm all right. We are now about 20 miles north-west of Kuwait city. You will know that 1 Armoured Division mounted a lightning attack from the 'Tri-Border Area', that is, where Iraq, Kuwait and Saudi join. While we lay in wait just south of the border all that time, false wireless messages were sent out by British warships lying off the Kuwait coast to deceive the Iraqis into thinking that the main thrust would be on the right flank, due north along the coast towards Kuwait City. Instead, we were many miles to the west. As you know, we struck straight into Iraq and then hooked east into Kuwait to cut off the retreating Iraqis, while the Americans surged due north to cut the Baghdad-Basra road, thus severing supply routes and cutting off the Iraqi army. The British Division travelled well over 200 miles virtually non-stop. Thank God it's over.*

Fusilier Palmer, Royal Highland Fusiliers,
1 March 1991

[Letter to Jane Watt] *Made it, thank God! Now we are in Kuwait we see the full ferocity of the Allied air attack, without which we could have suffered very heavy casualties. I have never seen such devastation... I sketched a dead Iraqi soldier on the Basra road immediately after the cease fire. He had a leg torn off below the knee, a severe head wound and most of his chest missing, but apart from that in very good order!! In fact I just felt a great sadness for the loss of life - a pathetic sight. There is no glory in this.*

Sunday 3 March PT in the morning with Captain Tony Hood's troop, which I found a severe strain! We played rugger, using a rock as the ball and a sand berm as the touch line. One soldier gashed his head on a boulder while scoring a try. Regimental church service for the whole Regiment; an historic occasion. Before the service Colonel Arthur Denaro explained the four points of the Divisional directive. In broad terms these were to: 1. Secure the area. 2. Clean it up, that is, centralize all Iraqi military equipment found. 3. Clean ourselves up. 4. Be prepared to present ourselves to the enemy, SEP [Surrendered Enemy Personnel], or visitors in good order. Colonel Denaro then led on with words to this effect;

> 'And now I want to say something heartfelt, because I'm an old campaigner and I'm allowed to. During this operation I have prayed every day for two things: that we would do our duty as well as anyone could imagine; and that we would take everybody back alive. At times I thought the latter was not possible. Others in the Brigade and Division have not been so lucky. The Staffords and the Fusiliers have both lost men. In our service we must remember them and their families. I thank God. I thank God for those who have prayed for us across the world; for those out here who have helped us; and I thank every one of you. And I am proud. Proud to command this team. I have been proud to see you train and proud to work with you. I was privileged and proud to go into that operation beside you... When I say *you* I mean every single one of you. You all contributed wherever you were on the battlefield, whether you had broken down at the FUP or were sitting at the A2... You may say, those who fought up front on the day, that it was easy. But at the time things were not easy because we did *not* know what the enemy would throw at us. What we *did* know was the array of NBC, artillery, and direct-fire weapons ranged against us. Whether you think it was easy or not you were courageous going forward into the unknown. On the day it was our standard of training that counted... It was our professionalism; our ability to adapt; our speed of reaction that made the whole thing easy.

> 'And I want to talk to you about another thing: your conduct has been of the very highest order. Your handling of POWs was correct and compassionate. Your decision on when to fire and when not to fire was correct. Our behaviour since we got here has been exemplary; and whilst we will go back from here without a personal trophy, because we have not scavenged and looted, we will all go back with something far better - our self-esteem, and with our heads held high. We will go back with pride that we have conducted ourselves well, we have done the job, and done it well. And we will go back with great friendships. We go back better blokes, more experienced and more considerate. We have seen the things that people do to each other, things we hope we never see again. But we must go back with humility and with patience because we go back into a different world where the pressures are different - the milk bill has not been paid - the 'Mrs' has damaged the car. Therefore we must go back with patience and hope that people will say: There is a *good* bloke, because that is what you all are - *good* blokes.

Went with Major Tim Bidie to the outskirts of Kuwait City. There I saw a scene of destruction the like of which *I* had never seen before nor wish to see again. Probably a thousand vehicles devastated by Allied air and ground attack, on a six-lane highway at the Mutla Ridge, north of Al Jahra on the Basra-Kuwait City road, and spread over a distance of about two miles. Artillery pieces, tanks, anti-aircraft guns, military trucks, enmeshed and tangled with civilian cars and buses. All had been pushed to the side of the road by military engineers and lay, six deep in places, at every conceivable angle - some hanging crazily on the edge of ravines or down embankments, or through fences, or upside down, or on one side. Others were buckled or jack-knifed, or blackened by fire. The contents of tanks and trucks were strewn

The Mutla Ridge, Kuwait, early March 1991

everywhere. Everything from clocks to clothing, cascading in a mad jumble from and between tangled wrecks and out across the road itself. Armies of scavengers picked through the devastation like crows on a rubbish tip: a sea of twisted metal, shell-cases, barbed wire, and metal fragments. Cables and live ammunition lay around amongst mattresses and refrigerators. A frilly white cotton dress fluttered in the wind, snagged on a vehicle hulk. The grey sand of the roadside verges was stained black with sticky patches of spilt oil, and the road itself was gouged and scorched. There seemed to be pieces of paper blowing about everywhere. Gutted buildings formed the backdrop, but groups of Kuwaitis moved down the highway in cars or on foot, apparently grateful to return to their devastated homeland. The highway itself was pock-marked by strikes from A-10 cannon. Everywhere were the signs of an army in retreat, loaded with loot and the *impedimenta* of war - a blend of chaos, devastation, and stench. Neither photographs nor pictures can ever fully describe such a scene, a panorama of

Wreckage on the Basra Road, early March 1991

destruction that goes beyond the limits of description and of peripheral vision. In every direction there was yet more destruction, but always too much for the eye to take in or for the brain to register. Probably just as well.[7]

Monday 4 March Walked two miles from Regimental Headquarters to a date plantation with Warrant Officer Dicken, 1st The Queen's Dragoon Guards, who was attached to QRIH as Intelligence Warrant Officer. *En route* we passed yet another abandoned Iraqi infantry position. Arrived at the plantation at midday. Bright green grass, row upon row of palms, and the unaccustomed sound of many birds. The latter were mainly small and included sparrows, some finch-like birds with black and white bars to their wings when seen in flight, and wagtails in profusion. There were also a large number of doves. If I recall a line from *Macbeth* correctly, it was bliss no longer to feel 'cabined, cribbed, confined', that is, hemmed in by camouflage nets and assailed by the constant buzz of human conversation, or the noise of wirelesses, generators, or engines. But amongst the rich greenery, it gradually became clear that this oasis was yet another abandoned Iraqi position, riddled with bunkers and strewn with wreckage and the paraphernalia of war. Even the wall that divided desert from cultivation had been wantonly destroyed. A black, white, and tan cat appeared and then disappeared into a ventilation shaft leading into a bunker. Three horses appeared from nowhere. They were all in a pitiful condition, with ribs protruding and heads hung low. One, a fleabitten grey, had sores on its haunches. They picked their way slowly through the palms. Curiously, they ignored the vegetation and chose instead to scavenge amongst the rubble, and then moved on.

I struck up a conversation with a Kuwaiti who was wandering, dazed, amongst the palms. He was the owner of this plantation and had just returned from the safety of Saudi Arabia. He told me that the Arabic name for this place meant 'the valley of the rotting corpses' which seemed sadly appropriate. According to local tradition, winter floods sweep down, drowning livestock in thousands. This place, which had at first raised my spirits, left me feeling empty and depressed. I was glad to leave behind the stench of decay and strike out into the open desert. Warrant Officer Dicken and I much enjoyed the unaccustomed freedom, quiet, and privacy as we re-traced our steps to Regimental Headquarters in the soft light of evening. My companion had found an Iraqi bayonet from an AK47 in a bunker and was in excellent spirits.

Tuesday 5 March A really foul day, with bucketing rain turning the sand to mud and forming large pools of standing water. I attended 'Morning Prayers' at Battle Group Headquarters at 0830 hours. Members of the 'O' Group team crammed themselves into the comforting co-coon of 'Zero Hotel' for the umpteenth time. This tent has represented an important link, however tenuous, with normal life. A six-foot table and wooden chairs; a few tattered copies of *The Field*, *Horse and Hound*, and *Country Life* stacked in the corner; even a framed photograph of Field Marshal Montgomery in the Western Desert,[8] faded but still imposing, hanging at an angle on the far wall. Those at the back of the group stood hunched against the elements, with *shamaghs* tightly bound and collars upturned to keep out the worst of the weather. Helmets have given way to berets and tent hats, although we still carry respirators. Everywhere there seemed to be good humour, broad smiles, and relief. Within the depths of the leaking tent was the unmistakeable figure of Colonel Arthur Denaro presiding over his team. It was during this 'O' Group that he made an instinctive remark that sticks in my memory. It seemed to indicate sheer relief that his dearest wish had been granted: the fact that he will now take back every man in his Battle Group alive. For me these words have a profound and, I suspect, lasting, ring which could well become a maxim for the future. At the end of the 'O' Group Colonel Denaro paused for a moment, leaning forward over the wooden table behind which he was seated. 'Remember', he said, 'Every day, *now*, is a *good* day'. The rain continued. I moved to A Squadron QDG [1st The Queen's Dragoon Guards] commanded by Major Hamish Macdonald. Towards dusk a fierce wind blew up. It continued buffeting the camouflage nets well into the night.

'The Date Plantation'. 1st The Queen's Dragoon Guards in action at Dhahr-al-Liyah, Kuwait, dawn, 28 February 1991

Wednesday 6 March The Prime Minister, John Major, addressed 7th Armoured Brigade, standing alongside Brigadier Cordingley on the front of a Challenger tank. Moved to the date plantation at Dhahr-Al-Liyah where I sketched a scene for a picture for A Squadron QDG [this was their final objective during Operation DESERT SABRE]. Returned to A Squadron leaguer on the engine decks of a reconnaissance vehicle. In the afternoon, sketched the profile of the Headquarters with the Union Flag and the Welsh Dragon aloft. That night, a jerboa came into the tent I shared with Hamish Macdonald. The jerboa sat between our camp beds on an open patch of sand. He was very tame. He groomed his cream and ginger fur and ate compo biscuits, his large eyes glistening in the half light of a paraffin lamp. He scuttled about under our camp beds most of the night.

Thursday 7 March Moved with A Squadron to a new leaguer area near Dhahr-Al-Liyah. Sketched an Iraqi T59 tank captured by the Squadron. The tank moved with the rest of the Squadron, crewed by the Squadron fitters and spewing thick black smoke. We crossed the Basra road at the exact point where the Irish Hussars had reached it one week earlier at the end of Operation DESERT SABRE. That event already seemed a lifetime away. We reached the new leaguer area and I sketched the Headquarters setting up. Men fought with billowing camouflage nets in a fierce wind. I then sketched the T59, head on behind a *bund*, with the muzzle facing straight at me.

Abandoned Iraqi T59 tank at Dhahr-al-Liyah, Kuwait, 1 March 1991

Friday 8 March. Went to the Mutla Ridge to make studies of the destruction. Made four sketches, including a general scene of burnt cars and lorries, the Police Post, and a T55 upside down with its gun barrel rammed into the ground. Finally drew a burnt corpse inside a vehicle, possibly an Iraqi intelligence officer, according to a Kuwaiti bystander. There were many documents strewn around the vehicle. There were two corpses in the car, but I only drew one. Only the back of the cranium and the lower jaw were intact. The jagged bones of the femur protruded. Both legs were severed above the knee. Fire had withered the torso to a charred mass, now the size of a child. The left arm was hardly recognizable, the hand shrivelled to a stump. The subject was the most difficult I have attempted. The corpse was lying on the floor of the vehicle because the seat had melted. A broken Kalashnikov, with only its metal components still intact, lay buckled beside the figure. The only way I could see the subject clearly was to lean deep inside the vehicle over the corpse itself. The stench of destruction hung in the air and its gritty, bitter taste seemed to catch in the throat. I draped my *shamagh* over the shell of the vehicle, to act as an awning to cut out the glare of direct sunlight, and to reduce the reflected light from wrecked trucks, guns, and tanks piled high all around.

The background to the carnage at Al Mutla is this: during the final stages of the Gulf War, elements of the Iraqi army fled in large numbers from Kuwait City, due north on the Kuwait-Basra road, a principal Iraqi MSR. The Coalition Air Force struck in the area of the Mutla Ridge at the Iraqis as they escaped in any vehicles they could lay their hands on. These ranged from tanks and military lorries to civilian trucks, buses, and cars laden with goods looted from Kuwait City. As the lead vehicles were immobilized near the Al Mutla Police Post by A-10s, traffic piled up behind and became targets for other aircraft and American tanks that now commanded the heights to the west. Furthermore, the Iraqis were unable to deploy in that direction because of an extensive barrier minefield laid by their own engineers. Most of those who managed to deploy into the desert to the east and west of the road were cut down. An estimated 1,000 vehicles were destroyed on a stretch of road measuring 2.4 kilometres. The number of Iraqis who died in this ghastly place is not known.[9]

Saturday 9 March Left QDG at 1030 and returned to QRIH. Two sketches, both of the debris of war. The first of an Iraqi tank HEAT [High Explosive Anti-Tank] round; the second of a hand grenade. Blustery day.

Sunday 10 March Spent a grim but successful day at the Mutla Ridge. Began to the north of the Police Post on a side road that runs west, where two corpses had been seen at the roadside the previous day by a captain of 22 Special Air Service Regiment. I found them more by scent than by sight. One had been killed while trying to escape on a motor cycle. The body was bloated, the face shapeless. I sketched the second corpse, an Iraqi soldier in combat jacket and trousers, lying face down. Little could be seen of the head except the back of it. The face was shrouded by a hood and the right hand, which was pulled in close to the side of the face like a claw, palm downwards with fingers spread. This soldier had probably died from a severed femoral artery. The saturated cloth of his combat trousers still glistened in the sunlight. The sketch, which I did standing above the corpse, was very difficult. It took one-and-a-half hours. At

Iraqi soldier, Mutla Ridge, 10 March 1991

midday an American burial team arrived to take the body away. The team had already buried about 400 Iraqis found strewn around the battlefield of Al Mutla. As the body was being moved onto a sheet it rolled over. It seethed with maggots. The American party pulled away in their truck to a grave nearby. The stench of rotting flesh had gone. The only indication that this was the point where a body had lain was a pile of maggots that would have filled a bucket. I covered them over with sand and was glad to be on my way.

This was a truly God-forsaken place, an impression emphasized by the sight of anti-helicopter obstacles that stretched to the horizon. The forest of tall, rusted steel poles reminded me, for a moment, of the hop fields of Kent or even the angled lances of Uccello's painting 'The Battle of San Romano' [in the National Gallery]. Some smaller devices, placed for the same purpose and shaped like the spokes of a wheel, were scattered haphazardly like sand-coloured sea urchins. And beyond, in the far distance, a long line of pickets snaked across this grim landscape, from the Mutla Pass itself to the heights to the west. The pickets marked the minefield by which some elements of the Iraqi army were hoist with their own petard, and the heights the point from which they were destroyed by American tanks. During the afternoon I made five small sketches. A lorry buried nose first in a crater, a T55 gutted by fire facing north, an upturned lorry on the crown of a rise with its wheels in the air, two trucks below a tall cliff, and a blackened burnt-out T62, set against the heights to the east. Finally, a sketch of a T55 facing north with Kuwait City in the background, barbed wire in the foreground, and clothing strewn as far as the eye could see.

At dusk I hitched a lift in a Land Rover passing north through the check-point near the Al Mutla Police Post, or what remained of it. The military and civilian team in the Land Rover I had not met before. They had flown into the recently re-opened Kuwait International Airport from England that very day and were *en route* to their destination. Their task was to analyse this or that. Travel-weary no doubt, they had hurried from Kuwait City and through the Mutla in failing

An Iraqi tank destroyed on the Mutla Ridge, early March 1991

light, apparently oblivious to the significance of this terrible place. I'm not sure if I pitied them or not. Nevertheless, I hoped that in the very act of drawing the scenes described that day, I had accorded one abandoned and unburied Iraqi soldier at least a trace of recognition, just one of many thousands who had been sacrificed for the greed of a repulsive dictator. I journeyed in silence with my own thoughts and in the hope that I might never see such a place again.

'Night on the Mutla'. Early March 1991

Monday 11 March Made a number of studies of Regimental Sergeant-Major J C Muir's Ferret scout car, *Tullyard* (Tullyard is a small village south of the city of Londonderry near Strabane). Included a sketch of a QRIH pennant.

It's quite late at night but who cares? It's finished and we wait to come home. I think the plan is we take the tanks back to Jubayl on transporters. They will then be shipped home, but crews will fly. I am working as hard as I was before this show. Sketching everything and anything. It is difficult to say how I feel: immensely relieved; amazed we are all in one piece except for minimal casualties. We are still in Kuwait. I wanted to go to Kuwait City to sketch but there has been such violence there that a curfew has been imposed and British servicemen are banned. But in any case the City itself does not come within the compass of 7th Armoured Brigade and I have seen enough violence for a lifetime. I never want to see it again. Not that anyone in their right senses would ever wish to see it in the first place. We are all heartily sick of destruction and desolation, and filthy weather and discomfort. I think we will be back pretty fast. 7th Armoured Brigade moves first. Every day now, is a good day.

Tuesday 12 March Arrived at the airfield in the DAA [Divisional Administrative Area] at 0930 hours.[10] By 1120 hours day had apparently turned into night and it was cold. Darkened figures clad in parkas huddled around petrol cookers and a few Land Rovers moved from A to B with headlights on. An oppressive blanket of oily cloud descended to the horizon in all directions, save for a single streak of dirty, acid-orange light which interchanged with dark grey bands of filth. The sun was reduced to a pale yellow-orange orb, surrounded by a faint orange glow similar to a full moon.[11] It was quite possible to look directly at the sun without flinching and to observe the variations in the tone of its surface. A Hercules transport appeared in the murk with all its lights on and, after a number of passes, managed to put down amidst a roar of engines and a huge cloud of dust. With the engines still running, we boarded and took off. We put down somewhere in Saudi Arabia and then drove by bus to a quarry where we spent the night. The tanks arrived by transporter in the small hours of the morning amidst the din of engines, shouted commands, and the clank of shackles.

Wednesday 13 March We rose before dawn. Crews began the process of removing slabs of armour, external fuel drums, and brackets for water cans. Photographed or sketched the following: *Aghadowey*, being taken off a tank transporter, and *Churchill*, flying an orange flag. Also sketched *Dun Laoghaire*; *Loughswilly*; *Coleraine*, including Major Nigel Beer unloading ammunition; and *Carlow*, flying the Union Flag and Irish Tricolour alongside each other. In the early afternoon I rode to the outskirts of Jubayl on the back decks of *Loughswilly*, commanded by Captain Richard Paley, in preparation for the final move to Camp 4. It was curious to think that the very tanks that now roared south in clouds of dust, along the palm-lined roads that converge on the city, were those that had been unloaded at the port of Jubayl the previous year, and had struck into Iraq and Kuwait across the Wadi Al Batin.

Thursday 14 March Visited the camel farm near the tank holding area at dawn. The owner gave me some camel milk. There were four camels in an enclosure: two adult females with two young ones. One of the young camels, a bull, was very friendly. His nose was soft as velvet and he nuzzled my *shamagh*. As I studied the camels in the enclosure more camels passed by, browsing on the salt bushes amongst date palms. At 1000 hours moved to Camp 4. I was pleased that my final view of the desert had been of camels and a camel farm, but it was strange how the taste of destruction still seemed to linger.

Camel study, Al Jubayl, 14 March 1991

Friday 15 March The flight from Dhahran to Brize Norton was delayed by 24 hours. This gave me the chance to sketch the two water-towers that overlook Camp 4 with palm trees in the foreground. The night was wretched, being hot and sultry. I hardly slept at all.

Saturday 16 March Made four studies of flowers, none of which I was able to recognize at the time. The first was crimson, with a very pale lemon flower half the size of a daisy growing inside the crimson, russet-gold, and violet-purple petals [bougainvillaea]. The second was very delicate with pale lemon inner petals surrounded by violet petals when viewed from above [lantana]. The third was the flower of a tree found at the end of long branches, hanging vertically rather like a willow [callistemon]. The flowers were scarlet-crimson, not unlike 'Red-hot

Water-towers at Al Jubayl, 15 March 1991

Poker', but more wispy and fine. Finally sketched a scarlet flower shaped like a lamp on a low bush [hibiscus]. At 1115 hours we boarded transport and left Camp 4 for the last time bound for the MCCP [Movement Control Check-Point] where my huge amount of luggage was processed. I was delighted to see the back of it. At 1530 hours we left the MCCP by bus for Dhahran. We passed innumerable groves of date palms and a number of villages. The houses and mosques formed interesting patterns, and most were whitewashed with clean lines. Then, quite suddenly, in front of us there was a city, with lights and life, green bushes and trees, and grass. Flocks of birds flitted about. Again quite suddenly, we were confronted by a vast white palatial building. It was a dazzling blend of modern and Arabian-inspired architecture, multi-faceted, ornate, and angular; with straight lines contrasting with sweeping curves. This was Dhahran International Airport.

At 1930 hours the Royal Air Force Tristar roared down the runway bound for Brize Norton. So ended my tour of the Gulf.

1   The squadron of tanks I saw on the move was B Squadron Scots DG. The squadron had been under the command of 1 Staffords for Operation DESERT SABRE and was moving south via the Irish Hussars to rejoin the Scots DG Battle Group, now established on the southern edge of Objective COBALT.

2   One Iraqi tank commander from 12 Armoured Division, reinforcing 49 Infantry Division, reported having 35 tanks under his command originally. Twenty-nine were lost during the air offensive; the remaining six were destroyed in ten minutes by artillery and tanks during the Allied ground offensive.

3   Another Iraqi soldier who walked for 20 hours in order to surrender had this to say on the subject of the physical and psychological impact of Allied air power: 'Twenty-four hours a day the planes shot. You can't imagine this.' This POW had apparently lived on two pieces of bread per day since the outbreak of the war (*Daily Telegraph*, 1 March 1991).

4   There were a number of reports of dogs feeding on corpses.

5   It was later confirmed that 24 British servicemen were killed in action and a further 23 died on active service from various other causes.

6   Iraq was reported to have lost 3,008 of its 3,600 tanks; 2,140 of its 3,200 artillery pieces; 1,857 of its 3,950 APCs; and about one quarter of its 700 combat aircraft, of which 100 were impounded in Iran. Iraq lost 41 divisions, either destroyed or rendered ineffective. Two armoured and two infantry divisions of the Republican Guard were broken in northern Kuwait or while retreating towards the Euphrates. The Tawakkulna Division was destroyed before the ground offensive began. It is impossible to estimate, even in broad terms, the number of Iraqi military personnel killed or injured, but a figure of 150,000 has been reported while 175,000 were captured. Allied losses in the land battle were USA 148, Great Britain 24, France 2, and Arab forces 50. The total numbers killed and wounded in action were 224 and 770 respectively.

7   The Iraqis had indeed paid a terrible price, but perhaps the phrase 'those who live by the sword ...' has never been more apt. Many of those caught in the trap had perpetrated heinous acts of barbarism against the Kuwaiti people. They had already demonstrated their capacity for vengeance to the revulsion of the civilized world, and their crimes against humanity and the environment are now well known. Even the animals at the Kuwait Zoo were made to suffer horribly at the hands of Iraqi troops. Some animals were reported to have been burnt, starved, eaten, or shot. As General Schwarzkopf was to say later, of Iraqi atrocities in general, '...the people who did that are not part of the human race' (*Daily Telegraph*, 2 March 1991). Invited by a news reporter to express his opinion of Saddam Hussein as a 'military strategist', General Schwarzkopf replied thus;

'he is neither a strategist, nor is he schooled in the operational arts, nor is he a tactician, nor is he a soldier. Other than that he is a great military man, I want you to know that'. (*Sunday Telegraph*, 3 March 1991).

8   It was curious to think that these were the direct descendants of the 7th Armoured Division, the Desert Rats, raised in the Western Desert in 1940, who fought in all the great battles of the North African campaign, including Beda Fomm, Sidi Rezegh, Gazala, Alamein, Tripoli, and Tunis.

9   It is important always to stress that the action by the Allies at the Mutla Ridge was no act of vengeance. It was an act of war against an army that had not yet capitulated and a loathsome dictator consumed by greed, who had inflicted war on a neighbouring sovereign state and his own people. Furthermore, the Iraqi army still retained much serviceable military equipment and the capability to regroup and support the Republican Guard, which was still putting up a determined resistance.

10 RSM Muir kindly drove me from the QRIH leaguer in Kuwait to the improvised airstrip in the DAA, somewhere in the middle of nowhere. It was a bumpy ride across the desert that took us through a vast and depressing quarry. At one point we bowled along a track running parallel to a pylon line. As objects stand out starkly against a bare horizon, our attention was immediately drawn to a wooden contraption built into the structure of one particular pylon about thirty feet above the ground. Closer inspection revealed the remains of an Iraqi observation post, probably for artillery. The structure had taken a direct hit. Most of the wooden planks and steel scaffolding lay in a heap at the base of the pylon but some planks still dangled among the steel girders, swaying in the wind. It seemed to epitomize the unworthiness of our foe or, more accurately, one rendered impotent by overwhelmingly superior tactics and firepower.

11 It was too dark to read a book at midday. According to one newspaper report the retreating Iraqis fired about 700 oil wells in Kuwait, burning an estimated six million barrels of oil per day or £40,000-worth every minute. Smoke was seen as far north as Baghdad and as far south as Riyadh. Reduced light caused temperatures to drop by ten degrees. The last of the oil fires in Kuwait was extinguished on 4 November 1991: the cost was at least £1 billion. The fire fighting operation was an international effort involving 27 teams from 10 nations. It was the Hungarians who captured the popular imagination by creating a devastatingly effective device to cap the wells using the blast from the engine of a MiG 21 fighter mounted on the chassis of a Soviet T34 tank.

CHAPTER FIVE
Postscript

Here I conclude with two main points. The first refers to a letter, written to the QRIH during Operation GRANBY by Mr E G Beckerley, a former 8th Hussar. The fact that this was written at a time of great need demonstrates clearly the fierce family spirit or clan loyalty that is the very foundation of the Regimental system of the British Army. It is this system and this spirit that has proved to be of such inestimable value over the centuries and remains so to this day, particularly in time of war. Mr Beckerley's letter also epitomizes the unstinting support of the British Nation for the British Forces serving in the Gulf, and the energy of that support will remain one of the abiding memories of the Gulf War, for those who took part in it.

Warrior, 1st Battalion, The Staffordshire Regiment, at Headquarters 7th Armoured Brigade, 6 March 1991

Dear Colonel Denaro,
As one of a group of 8th Hussars, I felt I must write to tell you, again, that our thoughts and prayers are with the Regiment at this time... It is now becoming increasingly likely that you will see action before very long; and the Irish Hussars, as ever, will acquit themselves well and prove themselves very capable of carrying out any task assigned them... Everyone is following events in the Gulf very closely, and we are fairly well informed - much more so than in any previous war. We all feel we are involved; the entire country supports our troops in the Gulf. There is a definite feeling that we are a nation at war. There is no doubt about the outcome, only a hope that it will end soon and that we can see you all safely home again. God-speed, Sir, to you and the Regiment.'

Against this background we were doubly saddened and dismayed to learn that the Government decision, announced on 24 July 1991, to make deep cuts to the structure of the British army, would be implemented. I shall leave the reader to guess my true feelings about this decision. My mildest reaction is one of pity. Pity for those who, so clearly, will never understand the incalculable value of the Regimental spirit and the comradeship it engenders on the battlefield. This is a privilege reserved only for the fighting soldier - a privilege which many ex-soldiers seek in the outside world for the rest of their lives, but never find. At the time of writing 40,000 soldiers are to be made redundant over four years. The cuts are to be achieved through the amalgamation or disbandment of many famous regiments, some of which served with great distinction in the Gulf War. Among them is The Queen's Royal Irish Hussars, to be amalgamated yet again, this time with The Queen's Own Hussars. The words of Colonel Denaro, commanding officer of The Queen's Royal Irish Hussars, epitomize the whole business; 'It is the saddest day of my military career. We will get on with the job but for one day at least we would like to be left alone with our sadness.' Another fine regiment, which also formed part of 7th Armoured Brigade, the Staffordshire Regiment, is to be amalgamated with the Cheshire Regiment. [This decision was later rescinded by the Government, due partly to unrelenting pressure from soldiers, former soldiers, and the communities of Staffordshire and Cheshire.]

My second point concerns the nature of war itself. In the days that followed Operation DESERT SABRE I thought it important to establish a balance to show that war, for all its hideousness, is not all misery and hopelessness. War has many facets, some of which, ironically and mercifully, give us cause for hope. There *can* be humanity. There *can* be dignity. There *can* be compassion and straightforward common decency, even between opponents. There was.

The following example records the selflessness of one Iraqi soldier and the restraint of his adversary. Following a preliminary artillery bombardment, tanks of The Queen's Royal Irish Hussars began to move forward onto Objective ZINC. The bombardment had been pulverizing, but necessarily so since the enemy position was believed to be large and strongly held, mainly by T55s. Challengers moved forward trying to pick up 'hot spots' in TOGS to indicate enemy vehicles or soldiers. The situation was confused. Would the enemy resist or surrender? Were the silhouettes of vehicles tanks, APCs, or lorries? Were they manned or unmanned? Were they static or on the move? Did they pose a threat and should they be taken out? If so, which ones? And the men seen in trenches. Would they surrender or were they preparing to fight? This was the dilemma that faced each tank commander. Amidst this confusion one tank commander spotted a solitary figure, a long way off, bearing a white flag. Unarmed, this man picked his way slowly forward in darkness from the defensive position he had occupied towards what is undoubtedly one of the most terrifying noises on the battlefield, the roar of massed armour at night. The desolation was compounded by the weather. It was a cold, overcast night with driving rain. This figure, a doctor it transpired, covered a distance of nearly a mile. That journey must have seemed interminable. At last he reached the line held by the point tanks. Beneath the gun barrel of a waiting Challenger he surrendered to its crew on behalf of his comrades.

It is not for me to comment on the detailed conduct of the operation on Objective ZINC. There were many tank commanders and others who were both better qualified to judge than I, and better placed to see. Nevertheless, it seemed to me from what I did see and hear, at squadron level, that this was an operation conducted with the utmost skill and professionalism. Its main features may be summarized as the forbearance of tank crews, the fine judgement and compassion of commanders; and the inspiration of the leadership, exemplified in the order for tanks not to engage the enemy unless he posed a threat but instead, to fire over his head to hasten his surrender. This was just one example but it serves, I think, to illustrate the fundamental respect for human life that must always lie at the heart of the profession of arms.

A Warrior of C Company, 1st Battalion,
The Staffordshire Regiment, training at Al Fadhili, 22 December 1990

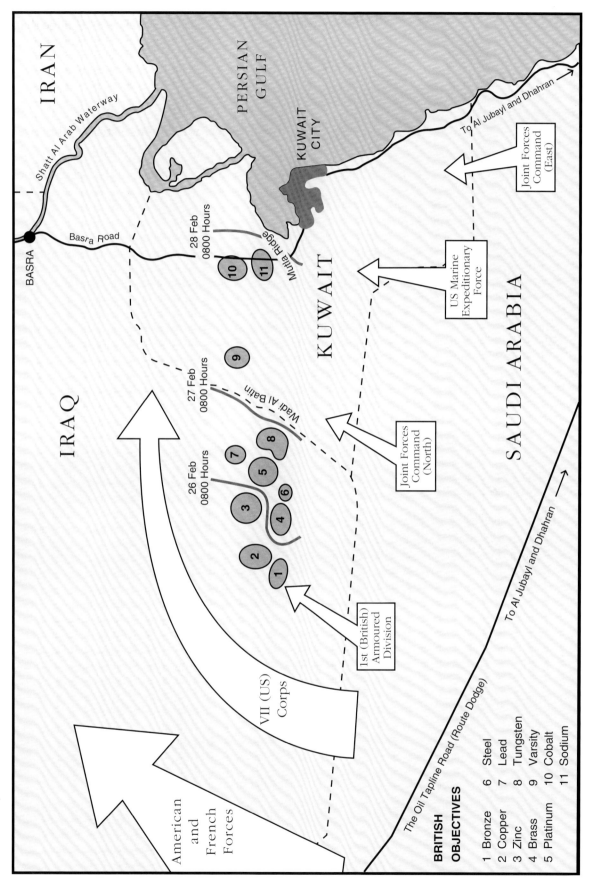

The Allied Ground Offensive: 24-28 February 1991

IRAN

Shatt Al Arab Waterway

PERSIAN GULF

BASRA

Basra Road

KUWAIT CITY

To Al Jubayl and Dhahran →

Joint Forces Command (East)

28 Feb 0800 Hours

Mutla Ridge

10 11

US Marine Expeditionary Force

IRAQ

9

27 Feb 0800 Hours

Wadi Al Batin

KUWAIT

26 Feb 0800 Hours

7   8

5

3   6

4

Joint Forces Command (North)

SAUDI ARABIA

2

1

1st (British) Armoured Division

VII (US) Corps

To Al Jubayl and Dhahran →

American and French Forces

The Oil Tapline Road (Route Dodge)

BRITISH OBJECTIVES

1 Bronze   6 Steel
2 Copper   7 Lead
3 Zinc   8 Tungsten
4 Brass   9 Varsity
5 Platinum 10 Cobalt
            11 Sodium

121

CHRONOLOGY

1990

2 Aug   Iraqi forces invaded Kuwait. UN Security Council Resolution No. 660 condemned the invasion and demanded the immediate withdrawal of Iraqi forces.

6 Aug   UN Security Council Resolution No. 661 imposed a range of economic sanctions against Iraq.

10 Aug   Arab League voted to back UN sanctions and send troops to help United States defend Saudi Arabia.

14 Sep   British Government committed 7th Armoured Brigade to the Gulf.

1 Oct   Lieutenant-General Sir Peter de la Billière appointed Commander British Forces Middle East.

22 Nov   British commitment increased to divisional strength with the addition of 4th Armoured Brigade.

28 Nov   Robin Watt flew to Al Jubayl, Saudi Arabia. John Major became the new British Prime Minister. No change in British Gulf policy.

29 Nov   RW moved to Camp 4. UN Security Council Resolution No. 678 authorized member states to use 'all necessary means' to enforce Resolution No. 660, unless Iraq complied with UN demands by 15 January 1991.

1 Dec   RW arrived at Headquarters 7th Armoured Brigade.

6 Dec   Iraq released British hostages seized in early stages of occupation of Kuwait.

6-20 Dec   RW visited medical, engineer, and support services of 7th Armoured Brigade.

21-24 Dec   RW visited 1st Battalion, The Staffordshire Regiment.

25 Dec   RW spent Christmas Day with The Queen's Royal Irish Hussars.

26-28 Dec   RW visited 40 Field Regiment Royal Artillery.

29 Dec   RW visited The Royal Scots Dragoon Guards.

31 Dec   RW moved with The Royal Scots Dragoon Guards from Al Fadhili to Abu Hadriyah, 70 kilometres north.

1991

1-3 Jan	RW watched live firing exercises at Devil Dog Dragoon Range, Abu Hadriyah.
4 Jan	RW returned to The Queen's Royal Irish Hussars at Abu Hadriyah.
6-7 Jan	7th Armoured Brigade conducted Exercise HOUBARA RAT, to practise live firing.
15 Jan	Expiry of final UN deadline to Iraq.
17 Jan	Start of Allied air offensive. Iraq responded by launching Scud missiles.
26 Jan	1st (BR) Armoured Division came under the tactical control of VII (US) Corps.
4-6 Feb	1st (BR) Armoured Division conducted Exercise DIBDIBAH DRIVE, to practise a Divisional move through a minefield breach.
14-15 Feb	1st (BR) Armoured Division conducted Exercise DIBDIBAH CHARGE, the final rehearsal for Operation DESERT SABRE.
24 Feb	G Day. Start of Operation DESERT SWORD, the Allied ground offensive.
25 Feb	G+1. Start of Operation DESERT SABRE, the British contribution to the Allied ground offensive. 1st (BR) Armoured Division, with 7th Armoured Brigade leading, advanced into Iraq.
26 Feb	G+2. 7th Armoured Brigade attacked Objective ZINC, and later Objective PLATINUM.
27 Feb	G+3. 7th Armoured Brigade reached Objective VARSITY, encountering only light resistance.
28 Feb	G+4. 7th Armoured Brigade reached Objective COBALT (the Basra Road, north of Kuwait City). Temporary ceasefire agreed.
6 Apr	Formal ceasefire agreement signed.
July	Final withdrawal of nearly all British Forces from Kuwait.

Order of Battle
1st (British) Armoured Division

Commander British Forces Middle East   *Lieutenant-General Sir Peter de la Billière*

1st (British) Armoured Division   *Major-General Rupert Smith*

Divisional Troops

16th/5th The Queen's Royal Lancers	(Armoured Reconnaissance, Scimitar)
2, 26, and 40 Field Regiments RA	(M109 self-propelled howitzer)
12 Air Defence Regiment RA	(Rapier SAM)
32 Heavy Regiment RA	(M110 self-propelled howitzer)
39 Heavy Regiment RA	(MLRS)
32 Armoured Engineer Regiment RE	
4 Regiment Army Air Corps	(Gazelle and Lynx helicopters)

4th Armoured Brigade   *Brigadier Christopher Hammerbeck*

14th/20th King's Hussars	(Challenger)
1st Battalion, The Royal Scots	(Warrior)
3rd Battalion, The Royal Regiment of Fusiliers	(Warrior)
23 Engineer Regiment RE	

7th Armoured Brigade   *Brigadier Patrick Cordingley*

The Royal Scots Dragoon Guards	(Challenger)
The Queen's Royal Irish Hussars	(Challenger)
1st Battalion, The Staffordshire Regiment	(Warrior)
21 Engineer Regiment RE	

For the sake of clarity, only some of the units of 1st (BR) Division are shown above. Other units serving included the following:

The Life Guards; 1st The Queen's Dragoon Guards; The Royal Corps of Signals; The Grenadier Guards; The Coldstream Guards; The Royal Highland Fusiliers; The King's Own Scottish Borderers; The Queen's Own Highlanders; 22 Special Air Service Regiment; The Royal Corps of Transport, The Royal Army Medical Corps; The Royal Army Ordnance Corps; The Corps of Royal Electrical and Mechanical Engineers; The Corps of Royal Military Police; The Royal Pioneer Corps; and The Intelligence Corps.

In fact, nearly every unit in the British Army provided some individuals for service in the Gulf.

SUGGESTIONS FOR FURTHER READING

Books

Bishop, Patrick	*Famous Victory: The Gulf War*, London (1992)
Brenner, Eliot and Harwood, William	*Desert Storm: The Weapons of War*, London (1991)
Brown, Ben and Shukman, David	*All Means Necessary: Inside the Gulf War*, London (1991)
Bulloch, John and Morris, Harvey	*Saddam's War*, London (1991)
Central Office of Information	*Britain and the Gulf Crisis*, London (1993)
David, Peter	*Triumph in the Desert: The Definitive Illustrated History of the Gulf War*, London (1991)
de la Billière, Gen Sir Peter	*Storm Command, A Personal Account of the Gulf War*, London (1992)
de la Billière, Gen Sir Peter	*Looking for Trouble: SAS to Gulf Command*, London (1994)
Hiro, Dilip	*Desert Shield to Desert Storm*, London (1992)
Micheletti, Eric and Debay, Yves	*Operation Desert Shield: The First 90 Days*, London (1991)
Moore, Mike	*Desert War: A Unique Photographic Record of the Desert Rats at War*, London (1991)
Pearce, Nigel	*The Shield and the Sabre: The Desert Rats in the Gulf War 1990-1991*, London (1992)
Pimlott, John and Badsey, Stephen (eds)	*The Gulf War Assessed*, London (1992)
Romano, Sergio	*Desert Storm: The Gulf War in Colour*, London (1991)
Schwarzkopf, H Norman	*It Doesn't Take a Hero*, London (1992)
Simpson, John	*From the House of War: John Simpson in the Gulf*, London (1991)
Smith, Graham (ed)	*Weapons of the Gulf War*, London (1991)
Taylor, Philip	*War and the Media: Propaganda and Persuasion in the Gulf War*, Manchester (1992)
Thesiger, Wilfred	*Arabian Sands*, London (1959)
Thesiger, Wilfred	*The Marsh Arabs*, London (1964)
Watson, Bruce *et al*	*Military Lessons of the Gulf War*, London (1991)

Articles

Aldred, Margaret · 'Lessons from the Gulf Crisis', *Royal United Services Institute for Defence Studies Journal* [*RUSI*], Vol 137 No 6 (Dec 1992)

Anon · 'Friendly Fire in the Gulf: Board's Findings', *Army Quarterly and Defence Journal* [*AQDJ*], Vol 122 No 1 (Jan 1992)

Anson, Sir Peter and Cummings, Dennis · 'The First Space War: The Contribution of Satellites to the Gulf War', *RUSI*, Vol 136 No 4 (Winter 1991)

Bark, Lt A M · 'Did the Gulf War demonstrate that War is still a necessary and effective instrument of Policy?', *British Army Review* [*BAR*], No 103 (Apr 1993)

Bolton, David · 'Did Saddam want War?', *RUSI*, Vol 136 No 1 (Spring 1991)

Boxhall, Peter · 'The Iraq claim to Kuwait', *AQDJ*, Vol 121 No 1 (Jan 1991)

Connaughton, Col R M · 'The Principles of Multilateral Military Intervention and the 1990-91 Gulf War', *BAR*, No 98 (Aug 1991)

Cordesman, Anthony · 'No End of a Lesson? Iraq and the Issue of Arms Transfers', *RUSI*, Vol 136 No 1 (Spring 1991)

Cordingley, Maj-Gen P A J · 'The Gulf War: Operating with Allies', *RUSI*, Vol 137 No 2 (Apr 1992)

Cordingley, Maj-Gen P A J · '7th Armoured Brigade: Commander's Diary - Part One', *AQDJ*, Vol 123 No 2 (Apr 1993)

Cordingley, Maj-Gen P A J · '7th Armoured Brigade: Commander's Diary - Part Two', *AQDJ*, Vol 123 No 3 (Jul 1993)

de la Billière, Gen Sir Peter · 'The Gulf Conflict: Planning and Execution', *RUSI*, Vol 136 No 4 (Winter 1991)

de Normann, Maj R · 'To war with the Press: some Recollections of the Media in the Gulf', *AQDJ*, Vol 121 No 4 (Oct 1991)

Denaro, Brig A · 'Leadership and Morale in the Gulf - A Regimental View', *BAR*, No 105 (Dec 1993)

Duncan, Col B A C · 'Cruelty and Compassion: an Englishman in Kuwait', *AQDJ*, Vol 121 No 2 (Apr 1991)

Duncan, Col B A C · 'The Gulf War: Echoes of Omdurman', *BAR*, No 98 (Aug 1991)

Hayr, Sir Kenneth · 'Logistics in the Gulf War', *RUSI*, Vol 136 No 3 (Autumn 1991)

Hughes, Lt-Col D P · 'Battle for Khafji: 29 Jan/1 Feb 1991', *AQDJ*, Vol 124 No 1 (Jan 1994)

Kay, Dr David · 'Iraqi Arms: Not ready for Inspection', *AQDJ*, Vol 122 No 4 (Oct 1992)

Khaled Bin Sultan, Prince · 'The Gulf War and its Aftermath: A Personal Perspective', *RUSI*, Vol 138 No 6 (Dec 1993)

McGill, Col I D T	'British Forces Kuwait in the Aftermath of the Gulf War', *BAR*, No 100 (Apr 1992)
Mack, Maj A R	'Women in Combat: The British and American Experience in the Gulf War', *RUSI*, Vol 138 No 5 (Oct 1993)
Monro, Col S H R H	'The Armoured Delivery Group 1st Armoured Division Op GRANBY', *BAR*, No 102 (Dec 1992)
Reid, Maj-Gen P D	'Tanks in the Gulf', *AQDJ*, Vol 121 No 2 (Apr 1991)
Roberts, John	'Oil, the Military and the Gulf War of 1991', *RUSI*, Vol 136 No 1 (Spring 1991)
Smith, Maj-Gen Rupert	'The Gulf War: The Land Battle', *RUSI*, Vol 137 No 1 (Feb 1992)
Thomas, C J D	'How Israel saw Iraq during the Gulf War', *RUSI*, Vol 136 No 4 (Winter 1991)
'Vox Militaris'	'The First Fifty days: Diary of the Iraq-Kuwait crisis', *AQDJ*, Vol 120 No 4 (Oct 1990)
'Vox Militaris'	'The Second Hundred days: Diary of the Iraq-Kuwait crisis', *AQDJ*, Vol 121 No 1 (Jan 1991)
'Vox Militaris'	'The Gulf War: Diary of the Final Sixty Days', *AQDJ*, Vol 121 No 2 (Apr 1991)

This list is necessarily selective. Further material may be found in *Soldier* Magazine and in the journals of the Regiments and Corps of the British Army who served in the Gulf during Operation GRANBY.

INDEX

National Army Museum Publications

The Armies of Britain 1485-1980

Follow The Drum

Butterflies & Bayonets: The Soldier as Collector

Tommy Atkins' Letters: The History of the British Army Postal Service from 1795

National Army Museum Year Book 1

1688: Glorious Revolution? The Fall and Rise of the British Army 1660-1704

The Road to Waterloo: The British Army and the Struggle Against Revolutionary and Napoleonic France, 1793-1815

Portraits for a King: The British Military Paintings of A-J Dubois Drahonet (1791-1834)

The Victorian Soldier: Studies in The History of the British Army 1816-1914

Lady Butler: Battle Artist 1846-1933

Against All Odds: The British Army of 1939-40

Touch and Go: The Battle For Crete 1941

The Forgotten War: The British Army in the Far East 1941-1945

Dawson's Army: From Libya to The Lebanon

Rex Whistler's War: 1939-July 1944: Artist into Tank Commander

Monty's Men: The British Soldier and the D-Day Campaign

The Gunners' Favourite: The 25-Pounder Gun: A Brief History

Project Korea: The British Soldier in Korea 1950-53

Ten Years On: The British Army in The Falklands War

Battledress Broadcasters: Fifty years of Forces Broadcasting (in association with SSVC)